WHEN
WOMEN BUILD
THE KINGDOM

Other Books by the Author

WHICH WAY IS HOME?
*The Diary of a College Student
Whose Parents Divorce*

NIGHT WRESTLING
*Struggling for Answers
and Finding God*

**SEDUCTION OF
THE LESSER GODS**
*Life, Love, Church,
and Other Dangerous Idols*

WHEN WOMEN BUILD THE KINGDOM

Who We Are, What We Do, and How We Relate

Leslie Williams

A Crossroad Book
The Crossroad Publishing Company
New York

The Crossroad Publishing Company
www.CrossroadPublishing.com

Printed in the United States of America

The text of this book is set in 11/15 Cochin.
The display faces are Nuptial and Calligraphic 810.

Library of Congress Cataloging-in-Publication Data
Williams, Leslie, 1951-
    When women build the kingdom : what we do, who we are, and how we relate / Leslie Williams.
      p. cm.
    ISBN 0-8245-2363-6 (alk. paper)
    1. Christian women – Religious life. I. Title.
BV4527.W5545 2006
248.8′43 – dc22

2006001357

ISBN-13: 978-0-8245-2363-3

For Stockton, my love

Contents

Contents

What Women Bring to the Table

In the middle of our current American gender reorganization, male/female roles have flip-flopped. Househusbands with working wives are no longer oddities; a "couple" no longer refers to a man and a woman; and the smorgasbord of opportunity for both men and women is so rich that it threatens to create identity indigestion. However, in spite of the hubbub on all fronts, one truth remains the same: women are different from men. We look different physically and our emotions and behavior are governed by a different set of hormones. Women were created equal but different.

Recent email wisdom makes this point with humor. If the three Wise Men had been three Wise Women, they would have (1) arrived on time because they stopped and asked for directions, (2) brought sensible presents, (3) made a casserole, and (4) cleaned up the barn.

One of my students, Angie Meyers, illustrated this point in one of her assignments. A man and a woman sit across a dining room table from each other. One piece of birthday cake separates them. Both seem unaware of its existence, but under those cool exteriors lies a deep yearning for cake.

Woman: "Are you going to eat it? Because I am just going to throw it out if you don't eat it." (She thinks to herself,

"Please don't eat it. I really want it but I don't want to look like a pig.")

Man: "I might. I don't know. I'm still pretty stuffed from lunch. I'll let my food settle a little and then I might eat it." (The man sits oblivious to the fact that the woman really wants the cake. He's full but thinks he could probably squeeze in another piece of cake without getting sick.)

Woman: "Well, I couldn't eat another bite. If you are going to eat it you need to do it now before it dries out. Besides, I need to wash the plate." (The woman thinks, "Make up your mind. Eat it or don't, but don't toy with me." She is getting aggravated: "Look at him, sitting there without a care in the world. He ate like a pig at lunch, and now he's going to take the last piece of cake!")

Man: "Can you just wrap it up so I can eat it in a few hours?" (He thinks, "I'm going to explode if I eat something else.")

Woman: "No, I will not wrap it up. If you want it wrapped up, you do it!"

(The man thinks, "I wonder where her hostility is coming from? Did I say something and not realize it? Did I forget her birthday, anniversary, Valentine's Day, Labor Day? Think! What did I do?") The man starts to sweat. What would make her freak out so quickly? He says, "Did I do something to make you mad?"

The woman is still eyeing the cake. (She wonders, "Why did I pick this moron? He is so selfish. Did he even ask once if I wanted the cake? Heavens no! What a jerk!")

Lightbulb moment for the man. He says, with caution, "Did you want the cake?"

The woman has had it. She is about to blow. (She thinks, "Why do I have to lose my temper for him to see his own selfishness? Of all the conceited things!") In a fit of rage she leaps across the table, grabs the cake, and stuffs the whole piece in her mouth. Spitting crumbs at the man, she says, "Eat that, Buddy!"

The woman walks out of the room with cake all over her face, leaving the man in his chair wondering what in the world just happened.

I rest my case. Men and women are different.

The best relationships between men and women require risking, venturing, delving into foreign territory — the mind of the opposite — in order to create something that transcends a squabble. As my husband, an Episcopal priest, says to those in premarital counseling, "Marriage is easy; it's eating breakfast together that's difficult."

For men and women in the church, working together is the difference between building the Kingdom of God and the Tower of Babel.

A theme running through Deborah Tanner's book *You Just Don't Understand: Men and Women in Conversation,* is that men relate vertically and women relate laterally. That is, on a first encounter with another male, men tend to assess their standing in terms of hierarchy — who is stronger, more intelligent, more dominant, or who has more power, status, wealth. Men are not comfortable until they have pegged each other in terms of a mutually agreed upon ladder.

On the other hand, when a woman first encounters another woman, she will often attempt to connect, to reach out, to find common ground — a place where differences in status, power, and so on are dispelled or equalized.

These are generalizations, of course. But it does explain why some men have a hard time asking for help in a hardware store or a car repair shop — admitting ignorance places the clerk above them in status. It also explains why some women will reveal personal things to a woman they barely know, thus establishing a connection outside a power structure.

To create a new metaphor for the male/female dialogue these days, I'd like to suggest that the differences in gender relationships form an intersection of the horizontal and the vertical: a cross. Both women and men are necessary to help build the Kingdom of God on earth.

This book explores the unique contributions that women bring to the work of the Kingdom. That first Easter morning, the men had closeted themselves planning what to do.

Reorganizing and reconnoitering were necessary in the face of their leader's death. However, in the ancient way of womanhood, the women chose an alternate approach. They knew what needed to be done in this tragic situation, and they walked together to the garden to perform the age-old ritual of anointing the dead. Because they were true to their natures, the women were gifted with being the first to see the risen Christ. They were instructed to pass the word to the men.

It's not about roles. In most mainline denominations, men and women alike are ordained: Men preach, teach, pray. Women preach, teach, pray. This book is not about performance or what women should and shouldn't do in church, but rather about the unique perspective, gifts, and attitudes that women bring to their preaching, teaching, and praying. It's also about the particular service women feel called to in the Kingdom's work.

We are all in it together. A man and a woman were paired on a retreat to teach a Bible story to second graders. The man insisted the best approach was to spell out the major points in the story. The woman suggested that the children might learn the story better if they acted it out. In the end, the woman led the children in acting out the story, and then the man reinforced the major points.

A man who joins a traditionally female-dominated organization such as the Altar Guild is liable to bring a freshness of perspective to God's work in preparing for the worship service — not because he folds the linen differently, but because he sifts the holiness, the reverence, the meaning of the task through a mindset otherwise focused differently.

This book looks at "women's work" — from preaching to making casseroles, from running a vestry to running a nursery. This book explores what we as women do to help build the Kingdom — who we are, how we relate to friends and family, and how we listen and respond to God's call in prayer.

These are our stories from the journey.

What We Do

Doing Lunch

You can never predict how the Holy Spirit will work over lunch. I don't know what men do over lunch — make business deals or talk about sports — but for women, lunch is an opportunity to connect. I remember lunches at McDonald's with a friend. We each had a preschooler and a baby. The older ones romped in the playscape, the little ones cooed and slept in their baskets, and my friend and I crammed as much real conversation as possible into the hour.

Maybe it has something to do with sitting down with someone over food, but doing lunch can offer a lot more nourishment than just the salad. In fact, it can save your life.

Karin from Alaska told this story. The treasurer at Karin's church had resigned, leaving the office in chaos. Karin recommended Denise, an accountant she knew to fill the position. When the church hired Denise, Karin took her out to lunch to show her the ropes. In discussing health insurance, something compelled Karin to ask, "How long has it been since you went to the gynecologist?"

Denise answered, "Seven years," and shrugged it off.

Karin kept at it. "Well, now you have new insurance with the church, so why don't you make an appointment?"

Karin kept bugging Denise until she decided to go see about a lump she had in her breast. It turned out that the lump was benign but growing too fast, so she made an appointment with a gynecologist. A week later she reported to Karin: she was riddled with cancer, tumors, and cysts. The doctor operated immediately and got everything. If she had waited, she would not have been as lucky.

Karin said, "The church literally saved Denise's life. Now she is attending confirmation classes. She has been loved and supported through everything, and has become an important part of our church community."

Karin's awareness of the Holy Spirit prompted her, giving her the courage to ask such a personal question over lunch. Women seem to have less reticence about getting to the heart of the matter in a short period of time — or maybe it's a different set of antennae about people. At any rate, Karin helped to build the Kingdom that day over lunch.

Not all lunches are lifesavers. Sometimes lunch is just lunch, or sometimes it's a good laugh, or a heart-to-heart among friends. Lydia was eating with three friends who were catching up with each other. Although she hadn't told many people, life had been tough at Lydia's household: Her teenage son had run away from home and lived on the streets for five days. Though he'd finally returned, Lydia felt ragged from the experience, and angry and grateful at the same time — angry that he'd run away and grateful that he had returned safely. She wasn't comfortable sharing her story because she saw so many of her friends' teenagers on the "right" track, being "normal." Yet she desperately needed someone to talk to. So this day at lunch, she ventured to say something to her group of friends, who had often prayed together.

Thinking she alone had undergone this trauma, Lydia discovered that two of the others had gone through similar experiences with their children and they had not shared widely either. Lydia said, "Now what are the chances of that? I was greatly encouraged."

Wynne told the story of a life-changing moment over lunch, something she wasn't even aware of until later. "I knew DeeDee from social stuff like the Junior League, but didn't know her well. Then I dropped out of the League and went to seminary to get a masters of arts in religion — not an ordination degree. Next thing I knew, DeeDee calls me on the phone and invites me to lunch.

" 'Wonder what she wants?' I thought.

"She picked this real cool restaurant by the lake, so we relaxed and ordered. Didn't take her long, though, to get to the point. She'd felt a tug to go to seminary too, but had some serious doubts. This was so weird. Two of us in a club that wasn't noted for its religious nature. Anyway, she bounced all sorts of questions off me and I was honest with her about what seminary was like. I didn't see her for a while after that."

Wynne paused. "After a year or so, I heard she'd enrolled in the seminary's hospital chaplaincy program. I also heard that she credits her decision to that lunch by the lake. You just never know how God works through you. I had no clue at the time."

When God's in charge using us as His instruments, sometimes we really don't have a clue at the time. Sometimes we never have a clue. Jane tells a "doing lunch" story that revealed God's hand through a chance encounter.

Jane was with a friend having lunch when an Asian baby wearing a crown streaked by her table, giggling. She was Princess for a Day. After her ran a Caucasian mother, who caught her up and hugged her right at Jane's table.

Jane said, "Oh, your baby is beautiful." Jane's daughter was trying to adopt a Chinese baby, and Jane wondered if this baby had been adopted.

The woman stopped and fell into conversation with Jane and her friend. She had indeed adopted her baby. The woman said to Jane, "Give me your daughter's name and phone number. I'm having a get-together for people who have adopted Asian babies."

The woman called Jane's daughter and she went to the party, where she met several different people who emailed her about an adoption agency in Colorado. Jane said, "Now here's the spooky part. The Chinese government allows only a small percentage of single women to adopt. My daughter is single. Once she began working with the agency in Colorado, she was accepted within twenty-four hours. She'd been working with another agency for months."

Jane discovered that the agency was started by a female Chinese lawyer and her missionary husband. Jane's daughter will go to China to pick up her baby within the year.

While listening to Jane's story, I was struck again by God's power and the amazing way He brings people together — and how even a casual outing can become a holy meal.

Right Place, Right Time

The movie *Apollo 13* pictured the earth from the perspective of the moon, with blue oceans, green continents, and swirls of clouds, a small sphere twirling and hurtling in its orbit. The cosmic view of God is so often lost among grocery lists, church squabbles, deadlines, and carpools, and we fail to see the big picture.

We also sometimes fail to see the connections. The same view of the earth from a distance doesn't show a major reality of twenty-first century life: the invisible communication network of phone lines, radio waves, satellite dishes, emails, and other transmissions keeping us in instant touch with people on the other side of the globe. If we could see this system from afar, the earth would look like an enormous ball of twine.

Another network, also invisible, is the Holy Spirit, traveling faster than the speeds of light and sound, circling the earth constantly, healing, comforting — and bringing people together in the right place, at the right time. This connectedness in the Kingdom defies definition and understanding, as the following stories illustrate.

Becky said, "I'd been active in our diocese for many years, but had just recently met a young woman who worked with the youth at the church camp. Last weekend, I was flying down to our diocesan council on a flight with no assigned seats. I was just about to sit down when I noticed this young woman sitting at the back of the plane, so I decided to join her. When I greeted her, she burst into tears. It turned out that she'd just gotten word that her father was dying, and she had to fly all alone to tell him goodbye. We talked the whole way. It was clearly providential that we were on the same plane. She needed someone to give her comfort during a difficult part of her journey, and God put me right there. The Holy Spirit is truly awesome."

Being in the right place at the right time can sometimes feel like an interruption in the flow of life. Kerry told this story: "My husband and I had a meeting scheduled for the following week with out-of-town guests when I received a call from my brother-in-law regarding my mom. Things were not good. My sister was tired of caretaking on her own and was at her wits' end. Two days later I was on a plane, but I knew I had to get back before the meeting."

When Kerry got to her mom's home, she was greeted by the disturbing picture of her mother, who'd been a pillar of strength and a role model for her, wringing her hands, repeating the same angry proclamations, refusing to take medication, and insisting that she had beaten this kind of thing before and she could do it again.

Kerry denied the severity of what she saw. She had to get home quickly and, besides, being the oldest child, she'd always found a quick solution to most problems. "Now, however, the more I tried to turn this woman around to the person I knew and loved, the more resentful, impatient, and frightened I became.

"Finally, after I changed my plans to stay longer and got over feeling angry at the interruption to my life, something happened. As I stood in the shower at the end of an exasperating, exhausting day, the realization hit me. I knew I couldn't be in two places at once, and I knew I had to stay with my mother because she was in serious trouble.

"In that moment of surrender, I felt bathed not only in warm water, but in a profound love. It was no longer about me but about what I could be in that moment for her. The next day, when my mother continued to run her fingers through her hair and rave the negative litany, it felt so natural to enfold her in my arms and just hold her. And my family is not one that shows affection through touching."

Kerry concluded, "That time with her gave me an opportunity to know her differently than I ever had before.

We are now living in a 'grace' period. Her life is once more meaningful and productive. What's more, the unfolding of this event brought my two sisters and me to a better understanding of how we want to be available to her in the future. What looked like a bad thing and a terrible interruption has had many gifts for all of us."

Wren's story illustrates how God can put the right person in our path at the right time, even in a place as unpredictable as a beauty parlor. Wren was an artist whose career had nosedived. No gallery would take her work, and she was rejected by juries for show after show. Wren said, "I felt like a cliché. I'd been working as a waitress for almost three years and had reached a very low point, wondering why I'd been given this so-called 'gift,' which clearly wasn't going anywhere.

"After yet one more rejection, I woke up crying. I begged and begged the Lord either to take the desire to paint from me, or to bring it to fruition. Miserable, I decided to cut my hair. My regular hairdresser was out, but I took the first available stylist — a really nervy thing for me to do.

"This woman I'd never seen before sat me in the chair. Before I could open my mouth, she said, 'Just a minute,' and went to the back. She came out with a picture."

At this point Wren interjected, "This was right after 9/11. The picture she showed me was the one with God in the sky with His arms outstretched over the Twin Towers as thousands of people ascended to Him. The picture really moved me and I said so.

"Then, she started talking as she cut my hair. Mind you, I had said nothing to her about my faith, or my struggles, or anything. She began telling me about a gift she'd been given, a gift she despised. Before she went to cosmetology school, she used to work the night shift at a nursing home. Every night, she would go from room to room, praying for the people in the beds. During her prayers, she began to get a feel for who was going to die soon. The longer this went on, the more distressed she became. Time after time, she would pray for someone and they would die. She had the clear sense that, in death, their healing was total; still, nobody wanted her to pray for their relatives anymore, and she became a frightening figure around the nursing home.

"Finally, she couldn't take it anymore. She begged God to take away this special discernment. He did. Now she cuts hair."

Wren said, "All this time, I'm sitting in her chair, practically with my mouth open at what this total stranger is telling me. She finished, 'Now I miss the gift. Maybe I wasn't right to pray for it to be taken away.'

"At this point, I opened up to her about the gift I no longer wanted, and how troublesome it was, how miserable it was making me. This hairdresser and I ministered to each other that day in a very special way. I have never seen her since. But I've never forgotten how the Holy Spirit brought

25

us together the day I decided to up and cut my hair." Wren concluded, "She helped me understand the nature of God's gifts at a deeper level. Sometimes a gift is a gift to others, but feels instead like a cross to the person with the gift. It's been several years now, and I can see why God gave me the gift of art. It's coming to fruition in an unexpected way."

In a variation on the theme of "right place, right time," a mother tells this story about her daughter, an art teacher, who was asked to illustrate the cover for the big diocesan worship service in October. With no clue of the passages to be used in the service, she decided to draw one of her favorite Bible stories from Luke.

Weeks went by, and the time came for the service. (To appreciate this story, it's important to know that in the Episcopal Church, the Scriptures are predetermined in the Prayer Book, so that the entire Bible is read over a three-year period.) At any rate, at church that morning, the Gospel just happened to be Luke 19:1–10, the story of Zacchaeus. The artist picked up the bulletin and showed the cover to her mother. There was Zacchaeus in the tree and Jesus riding by on a donkey. Without knowing it, she had illustrated the Biblical lesson for the day.

Coincidence? I like to call it God-incidence. If we remain attuned to the presence of God, many times when we simply show up for our daily assignments, it is at the right place at the right time.

The Bible from a Woman's Point of View

As the authoritative Word of God, the Bible speaks to each of us, whispering, shouting, teaching, comforting, and confronting us wherever we are in our journey. The mystery of this book is that we can read the same text over and over and never plumb the depth of meaning. For example, the story of Jesus' passion touches and teaches us something new every year, revealing God's love in whatever we are going through at the time.

Though the Word is unchanging, we are not. We are in process, growing as we continue to dig for meaning in the Bible. What we bring to the Scriptures in prayer helps to determine what God reveals to us in his Word. Because women are different from men, what we bring sometimes provides a different perspective. For instance, men and women can both relate to, say, Peter. We can all find times in our lives when we have denied Christ. We relate to Peter in our human nature. However, in passages like the Abraham and Sarah story, I find myself wondering what the situation was like for Sarah. We aren't given much information from her point of view, but the day that Abraham set out with Isaac for a three-day hike . . . well, I wish the Bible had included Sarah's prayer for her child's safety that day, and maybe a lesson on trusting your husband as well as God.

Reading the Bible with a group of women helps us interpret the Word as it applies to our circumstances. Tammie tells this story of how a girlfriend helped her understand a Bible scripture that Tammie's mother had bludgeoned her with for many years. "Sometimes I think you've gotta know Mom to believe her. Dad always said she'd have been good in the army as a general. She's got an opinion — the correct opinion — on everything. And she uses the Bible to back it up. Her favorite is 'Children, obey your parents.' So going against Mom can sometimes not only upset the family battalion structure, but risk the wrath of God. 'Obey your parents' was the dictum at our house, whether it had to do with personal finance, child rearing, religion, or politics."

Tammie continued. "As the years went by, I became bolder. Mother would ask us as older children to do unacceptable things ('Take my urine specimen to the lab. Show me where you bruised your bottom in athletics'), and I put a quick end to it.

"But I always felt guilty. 'Children, obey your parents' rang in my ears.

"One day, I related this trait to a close friend, a better Bible student than I am. She asked, 'You never read the rest?'

"I said, 'No,' and went to look it up. There it was in plain English, in a reliable translation: 'Fathers [and presumably mothers] do not provoke your children to anger.'"

28

Tammie's mother/daughter guilt had been alleviated by Scripture, through the wisdom of a friend. She learned that passages should not be lifted out of context selectively, especially when they are used for personal control issues.

Sometimes the Bible speaks to us in the deepest level of our being. But sometimes it speaks to us on a direct level, too. Joanna tells this story: "Walking had become a passion for me — just short of an obsession. Every morning I would walk and recite a prayer I learned at a retreat, a paraphrase of Psalm 16. I loved my quiet, brisk walks with God but my hip started to hurt so I was walking less and reading the Bible more. For weeks, when I would 'randomly' scan a passage, a recurring theme kept revealing itself: 'Walk the straight path, the level way; choose the right path and walk in it.' These words resonated in a variety of ways.

"I searched and searched my soul, journaling to try to figure out where I needed to correct my path of life. Did I need to change my approach to God, my focus?

"In the meantime, I was getting frustrated at not being able to walk without pain, so I finally saw a chiropractor. He x-rayed, poked, and adjusted my pelvis to align properly. He asked where I did my exercise and told me to be sure to walk on the sidewalk or on a track to keep my spine aligned. Apparently the fact that I tended to walk on a sloped street was causing one leg to lengthen."

Joanna concluded, "It didn't take long in this adjustment to realize that all the messages I had been getting from God were literal: *Get on the level path.* "

Sometimes the Biblical message isn't mysterious at all!

Jean told a story about the response she got when she asked the Lord for a scripture to meditate on: "One evening He led me to Matthew 2:11, in which the Wise Men found the Christ child with Mary. They fell down and worshipped Him, opening their treasures of gold, frankincense, and myrrh." Jean thought and thought about this scripture, reading it over and over. Finally, she asked, "What do You want me to see here, how can I give the baby Jesus gifts?"

She heard, "Whenever you feed the poor or help another, you give your gold. When you worship, praise, or thank Me, you give your frankincense. When you weep for the lost and dying, you give your myrrh. You can give to Me as much as you want, as often as you want; it is up to you."

Jean realized that we don't have to give fancy gifts to Jesus. Building the Kingdom is simpler than that. Compassion, worship, and helping others are the building blocks.

One college professor starts every semester by telling her students, "I expect to learn a great deal from you," and she is never disappointed. When we teach, we learn. In the Biblical discussion of gifts of the Spirit, teachers are third in rank, after apostles and prophets (1 Cor. 12:28). Teaching is important Kingdom work.

Whether we feel anointed or not, we women often find ourselves in the role of "teacher." Women teach each other how to burp a baby, how to make Hollandaise sauce, how to recover from grief, how to start dating again, how to maneuver in the job world, how to crochet — not to mention trying to teach our children everything from manners to spirituality.

Teaching the Bible is a gift of the Spirit. Sometimes this gift is part of the equipment we are born with; sometimes it lights on our heads like a butterfly for a specific situation. Penny told this story: "The leadership committee asked me to teach on Revelation 4. I did *not* want to be in the position of lecturing before hundreds of women, and I begged God in my prayer time to give this task to someone else. But I also prayed for His will to be done.

"When it turned out that, indeed, God (and the committee) had picked me for this task, I buckled down to work. The Lord both directed and inspired me as I prepared and gave a lecture on what Heaven is going to be like. I described taking our crowns and laying them at Jesus' feet, praising Him, and dancing on streets of gold. By the grace of God, I got through it." She paused. "But that's not the half of it."

Penny continued. "One month later, my son died suddenly. With no preparation, we had to deal with this terrible tragedy. After I received the news, I staggered into my bedroom and saw on my desk the lecture I had given on how it's going to be in Heaven. It was as though God spoke directly to me: 'I have your son with Me. He does not need these words now, but you do.' When I gave that lecture, I had no idea what it would mean to me later on."

As the Word of God, the Bible is an individualized instruction manual and a source of comfort for everyone; as women, we have the opportunity to drink deeply — and pass the cup.

✦ *Funerals as Going-Away Parties*

The funeral service in the Episcopal Church is a special form of a going-away party, a celebration of the life of the person who has died. The service focuses on rejoicing over the deceased person's new life in Christ, and is often followed by a reception.

The word "reception" has a special meaning when it comes to funerals. On the one hand, it's a party when the family "receives" the good wishes of their friends, but on the other it's the occasion when the deceased is "received" into the Kingdom. The reception provides a transition for the family between the final farewell at the graveside or columbarium, and going home to an empty house. It's a time when mourners hug each other, tell stories, and remind each other that death does not have the final say.

A funeral reception is an earthly reflection of the party going on simultaneously in Heaven. While our event is tinged with sadness, the party in Heaven is filled with joy.

Maybe it's because women are active participants in life as it begins, but we seem to gravitate toward roles that help ease the transition into death. Women are involved in hospice, women prepare the altar for the funeral service, women often bring a casserole to the family, and women put on funeral receptions. Men participate too, but even in this age of role reversals and liberation, women still seem to play an elemental part in the rites of death.

Lucinda tells this story: "My friend Valeria was in charge of funeral receptions and, for some reason, people started dying in our church at an alarming rate. We had a large congregation, but still we had a freakish number of funerals during a particular eighteen-month period — fifty or more.

"Valeria never complained, but one week she had to put on four receptions, and I could tell she really needed some help. By God's grace, I had a break in my schedule, so I signed up to be her assistant during this time.

"What a blessing that experience was! Valeria and I became very close as we sliced tortilla wheels, made chicken salad, stuffed deviled eggs, arranged cheese platters, arrayed vegetables, and organized fruit trays. Valeria believed that every reception should be beautiful as well as delicious, so she added touches like lace and roses and unique centerpieces.

"I remember one reception for an older woman. Her family attended another church, but Valeria, as usual, went all out for the reception. A friend of the woman came up to Valeria and thanked her. 'In fact,' the friend said, 'This reception is so lovely, I'd like you to cater my next party.'

"With a twinkle in her eye, Valeria said, 'Thank you for your gracious compliment, my dear, but I only do funerals.'"

Lucinda continued, "It's a cliché to call it 'a woman's touch,' but Lucinda sensed that it made a difference not to plunk down tasteless food in tacky containers. A funeral reception, like a wedding, is a once-in-a-lifetime event, a real memory-maker for family members — and she wanted to send the deceased home in style. When the budget didn't allow fresh flowers, she would pluck a branch from one of the shrubs."

It's the plucked greenery, the small touch that women contribute to the big events in a church's life.

When funerals are done properly, God is alive and well in the midst of the congregation. Women I interviewed told me some amazing stories of funerals they had been a part of. Margaret said, "The son of one of my dearest friends died in a tragic accident. This family was much-beloved in our community, and the church was packed with people. I sang in the choir for the service and spent most of the time praying for my friend to make it through. I don't know how any mother could go through a funeral under those circumstances without the help of the Holy Spirit.

"One of the songs we sang was 'On Eagles' Wings.' When I looked out over the ocean of clothes, I saw my friend's face standing out like a lighthouse among the black and navy blue. She was incandescent with radiance. Her face took my breath away. I went up to her at the reception and said, 'When I saw you, your face was like a candle in the darkness.' She replied, 'All I know is that I was lifted off the pew with a sense of overwhelming peace.'"

Penny spoke of a similar experience after her father died. She had watched her mother tend to her husband in his last days. Strong and obedient until the end, her mother inspired friends and hospital workers alike. When her father finally passed away, Penny asked God for a gift at the graveside, something special to reveal His presence. First she asked for a rainbow, but then realized that a rainbow meant rain and that would put a damper on the outdoor ceremony. So she asked God for the presence of a butterfly.

Penny wasn't even sure why she said that prayer. Neither she nor her mother needed a sign. Yet, up bubbled the prayer request in a moment of closeness with God.

Penny said, "At the graveside, in the middle of the eulogy, a huge monarch butterfly flew in out of nowhere. It landed on the casket, matching the flowers on the top. It paused there, and then flew away. There wasn't another butterfly in sight." Every once in a while, God gives us inklings of His presence in times of sorrow, a brief foretaste of the celebration to come.

Laurie told a story about when she was first ordained in the Episcopal Church. Scheduled to participate in the funeral service of an older woman, she discovered that God had a different role in mind as well. Laurie was assisting Tom, another new priest, for his very first funeral. The two priests had made their way up to the front of the church when an older gentleman keeled over in the pew with a heart attack. He was the father of the dead woman's daughter-in-law. Tom ran to call 911, and everybody else was just standing around, staring. So Laurie began CPR, continuing until the ambulance arrived.

The man's daughter was distraught and torn. "Should I stay for my mother-in-law's funeral, or go to the hospital with my father?" Tom advised her to go with the living. The woman rode in the ambulance with her father. Although her father died shortly after arriving at the hospital, by performing CPR, Laurie had been able to keep him alive so his daughter could ride with him and tell him goodbye.

One priest's wife said, "I just hate funerals. They always happen on my husband's day off, and he's too sweet to ask them to change the day. And because we're in a huge church, the phone rings off the wall with frantic people asking me questions I don't have the answers to (No, I don't know where the extra candles are kept; I don't know who the scheduled acolytes are; I don't know whether the choir is singing or not). In fact, I try not to answer the phone when someone active in the church has died. I help the best by staying out of the way.

She continued, "But I have to say that occasionally the Lord has used me in dealing with family members. The first time was several years ago, when a family member called and my husband was gone. She was desperate to talk, and I listened. I didn't have a clue what to say, so I prayed while she talked. I guess an untrained ear is better than no ear at all when you're upset. After that, I've talked with several people in distress, and I'm not so nervous anymore about what to say. I just pray and listen."

The growth of hospice has helped ease both the dying and the family members into the new reality of death. One woman, Laina, helped establish hospice in Vietnam, and has done remarkable work as a missionary there for ten years. She worked in Ho Chi Minh City (downtown Saigon), traveling back and forth to her flat on a motorbike. She said, "One night, I decided to vary my daytime route and go home by way of better lighted streets. But I automatically turned down the usual path onto a very dark street. As I was riding along, I found myself surrounded by prostitutes. There were so many — some very young and frightened, others pregnant, and others pros. Their pimps were on motorbikes at either end of the street. I slowed down and began to pray for each one as I passed by.

"The next day at breakfast I asked a friend who had been in Vietnam for a long time whether any organization was working with these women. She said there had been in the past, but currently they had no help. I began praying each day for these women."

Laina continued, "Two weeks later, I was speaking at an HIV hospital and one of the physician assistants asked me to join a small group the next day. The group had identified HIV-positive men and was working with prostitutes. Another volunteer on the hospice project and I began holding classes for the men on each Wednesday and for the women on each Saturday. For nine weeks, we taught the women how to care for themselves, how to give themselves breast exams, how to watch for STDs and signs of cancer, and the importance of using condoms even if their clients wanted to pay more not to. The HIV-positive men had all been rejected by their families and employers. We taught them to take care of each other when they became very ill. We called the group 'Friend to Friend.' Many stories of family reconciliation came as a result."

Laina concluded, "Later, we worked with a group of nuns and developed a whole hospice village for HIV/AIDS families. Many of the men we worked with have died, but through them we were able to develop a cottage industry at two of the hospices to keep their families from becoming destitute, giving them jobs and a place where the children can go to school. Sometimes faith like a mustard seed can move mountains."

Sooner or later, death visits every house, all over the world. As Christians, we are blessed to see death not as the end, but as the beginning. As women, we build the Kingdom by listening, praying, and being present to help ease the transition from life to life.

Food, Food, Food

Three women died and went to heaven. St. Peter said to the first woman, a Baptist, "Why do you think you should be admitted?" She replied, "Because I've read my Bible every day of my life." St. Peter let her in.

He asked the second woman, a Roman Catholic, the same question. She replied, "Because I've said my rosary every day of my life." St. Peter opened the gate.

The third woman was Episcopalian. "Why do you think you should be admitted?" She replied, "Here's my casserole."

The joke doesn't say whether St. Peter let her in or not, but faith and food have a definite correlation. What soup kitchens, baptismal receptions, church picnics, and weddings have in common is the gathering of the community of faith, doing something crucial in Kingdom building: feeding sheep. It's not just ham and potato salad at the potluck after the Easter service, it's a foretaste of the heavenly banquet, and the Holy Spirit moves through the crowd like a cool breeze.

After all, the first communion services were full meals.

Wynette tells the story of how one woman used her creativity to feed her church of almost 1,000 members with no kitchen. "Our church tore down the old parish hall kitchen and it was going to take at least a year to build the new one. In the meantime, we had a sink, period, in the Sunday school wing. No stove, no dishwasher, no oven, no pots and pans. Since we'd been having a Wednesday night program and a meal for years and years, people expected to arrive at church and find some food to go along with their study classes. What to do?"

One woman stepped forward to handle this challenging situation. Barbara had owned and operated a restaurant for many years and she knew how to think outside the box. She brought in several turkey roasters and made soup. As Wynette said, "Week after week, we ate the most delicious soup you've ever tasted. Barbara also brought different kinds of bread, crackers, tortilla slices, and desserts and the church feasted for months. She worked miracles out of a tiny counter space and a sink."

Women are also in charge of the smaller, individual food events in the life of the church. Committees — formal or not — arrange for food to be delivered to the homes of shut-ins, new babies, sick people. Dianne tells this story to illustrate her belief that one of the primary ways women reach out to others in the Kingdom is through food. The mother of one of Dianne's son's friends underwent surgery for breast cancer. Women galvanized into action, making lunches for her children and bringing supper every other night. A cooler sat on the front porch, and women dropped off all kinds of meals in the cooler so the recovering woman wouldn't have to get out of bed to answer the door.

Another one of Dianne's friends underwent neck surgery and had to wear a neck brace for almost six weeks. With three children and a wild schedule, she was lost before her friends stepped in to carpool, cook, and help. The woman experienced freedom from worry because she had a clear sense that the Lord was providing for her through her friends. Dianne said, "One day, she was at home and didn't have any lunch. Just then the doorbell rang, and a friend had brought her some tuna fish. Her brother was not a Christian, and he was overwhelmed watching her Christian friends in action. He couldn't believe it."

Dianne continued, "Women have a sixth sense about the details of each other's lives. We know what needs to be done. When someone's life is thrown into crisis, one important thing is that we pray. Sometimes we go over to their house and pray with them. Then we get to work and help bear their burden — and it's a joy to help."

Caroline told an Easter story in which a change of focus and a dish of bread pudding brought their own resurrection: "Easter Sunday morning I woke up really tired from a

41

trip to Puerto Rico. I was low on thyroid, out of estrogen, swollen, exhausted, plus I had a killer headache. I was trying to make bread pudding with a yummy sauce to take to Easter brunch at church, and everything kept going wrong. I was making colossal messes and the pudding sauce (very time-consuming and expensive to make) turned into brown cottage cheese. *Yuk!* I screamed, 'I can't take it any longer! I hate being a screw-up and I'm sick of not being able to do anything right today.'

"I told my husband that I wouldn't be going to church this morning, Easter or not. I felt like a failure and couldn't be a phony trying to act nice, normal, and together. He went on to the early service without me. I sat at the computer mindlessly playing games, still distraught and bellowing, with my heart racing — when thoughts began to whisper in my mind, 'There, there, it's all right. It's all right, it's all right, there now, shhhhh.' This went on for a few minutes until I was aware of the ugliness and anger beginning to seep out of me. My pounding heart and head quieted, and my sobs lessened. Calming down I felt like I was floating. There was something so smooth, something soft, velvet inside."

Caroline continued. "It was God. Suddenly, I was totally peaceful, sitting here smiling and breathing slowly. I noticed what a beautiful day it was — *Easter!* After basking in the silence a while, I heard God's Spirit in my mind again, so loving. 'It's not about you. It's about *Me*, wanting to care for you, heal your spirit, be a balm to your mind, take care

of you because of what you can't care or do for yourself.'
What comfort!

"I got up with the biggest sense of relief I've ever experienced. I got ready for church, took that bread pudding
without any sauce, and it was just fine. It wasn't about food
not turning out, or my big hissy fit, hormones, or anything;
it was about God calming the raging storm within me and
tenderly comforting me. His presence tore through darkness and brought peace. I'd been resurrected from hell, and
could celebrate Jesus in a way I never could before."

Sometimes we get caught up in making the perfect dish,
especially for church, because we want it to be an offering of
our very best. And yet, the food is not what really matters.
One prayer group realized that they had gotten caught up in
a food competition, and members became reluctant to host
the group because it had turned into a production of food
instead of prayer. They agreed to forget the food altogether
and serve water, to the relief of all the members.

As women, each of us has to come to terms with is the fact
that our grandmothers and mothers cooked as part of their
job descriptions. But these days, we are no longer enslaved
as cooks. Entertainment too has changed over the decades.
Used to be, growing up female meant you were expected to
be a hostess — especially in terms of helping hubbie up the
corporate ladder. Now America goes out to eat and many
husbands participate in cooking for the family. Yet the stereo-
type of the woman as the family's social chairman lingers.

The gift of hospitality is like any other gift from God. Some have it and some don't. Each of us has her own comfort level with having people in our home — and whether or not we feel called to open our doors. Entertaining is no longer a *de rigeur* woman's activity; like singing in the choir, teaching Sunday school, or volunteering for the outreach committee, entertaining should be undertaken only when called — and feeling guilty is not part of the equation!

Marty's husband was a doctor when they married; now he is a minister. In the early days of their marriage, Marty entertained frequently, with enthusiasm. "I just love to cook," said Marty. During seminary and her husband's first two positions as minister, she continued to entertain all kinds of groups, including the church as a whole.

Then she got a full-time job and no longer had the time or energy to entertain. Her husband acknowledged the situation, and took up the slack by finding a caterer and making all the arrangements himself. Marty said, "I had some serious burnout, as well as guilt. All I could do was show up, smile graciously, and help him clean the kitchen." When they moved again and Marty got a part-time job, she resumed her role as hostess. "I got back my enthusiasm for opening our home." She paused. "Sometimes you're the dishwasher, sometimes you're the cook. And sometimes, I've been too flat tired to do anything, and we've taken the bishop out to eat instead. It doesn't matter — it's all for God."

Rolling with the punches is an essential part of the gift of entertaining. Alexandria told the story of a woman who hosted a potluck for her sixteen-member bridge group. Every single woman brought a lemon meringue pie. What else can a hostess do but laugh, serve pie, and pass the story on?

Celeste, a gracious and gifted hostess, expressed her views of entertaining, saying, "You reveal your soul when you entertain. You share yourself with others. It doesn't feel like work when it's a ministry." She went on to tell two stories about God's stepping in to help in specific ways. Right before her annual open house for 150 people, Celeste's daughter sloshed the chili con queso all over the kitchen floor — just as the first guests rang the doorbell. Celeste said, "Oh, God, please help." As if on cue, her husband went to the door and kept the guests talking in the foyer long enough for her to scrape the queso off the floor and into the disposal. God took care of the problem.

Another time, Celeste had set the tables for her forty guests. When the guests started going through the buffet line, she noticed that she had forgotten all forty napkins. She called over her son (ten or eleven at the time, and now an Episcopal priest) and said, "How would you like to earn five dollars?" Her son took the napkins and, with great aplomb and flourish, spread one on each guest's lap. Celeste said that the guests thought it was all part of the plan and that the individual attention made them feel extra special.

Another woman, Renee (a minister's wife), told a story from her perspective as guest rather than hostess. She realized that part of her role in Kingdom building had to do with others' parties. Renee was an extreme introvert. Big parties were anathema to her. She felt overwhelmed by all the smiling faces. She couldn't remember people's names. She never felt well-dressed. And someone always caught her with a mouthful of food, so she couldn't even eat comfortably. She arrived home exhausted.

Renee said, "The first Christmas after my husband entered the ministry in a large parish, we received fifty million invitations to parties. It seemed like every night for the whole month of December one parishioner or another was having a party, sometimes two or even three a night. Babysitting bills were setting us back, and I dreaded evenings that Advent."

Renee said she couldn't remember when it hit her, but she was sure it was one night when she collapsed into bed with sore feet. She suddenly recognized that these were parties, not torture — designed for celebration and fun. The church was thrilled to have her husband as a minister, and in their joy the parishioners wanted to include them in their homes. Maybe Renee's role was to let them.

From that point on, Renee felt called to attend her church members' social events as part of her own ministry. "Just showing up at people's parties is a form of blessing." As is so often the case when we're obedient, parties became easier for her, and she confessed, "Sometimes I even have a good time now."

Entertainment as a ministry doesn't just include having parties for adults. Sometimes entertaining our children's friends is an important aspect of Kingdom building. One woman said, "Even when the kids were small, I kept a snack basket on top of the refrigerator, so all the neighborhood children could feel at home in our house. Then, when the kids were teens, I stocked frozen pizzas and cartons of soft drinks, so at least I'd know where my children were hanging out."

Each one of us has to decide prayerfully how entertainment plays a role in our ministry. Fortunately, in this day and age, we can dash to the nearest pastry shop and put delicious delicacies on our own platters, smiling graciously when someone compliments the petits fours. "They are heaven-sent" is always a good reply when someone asks for the recipe.

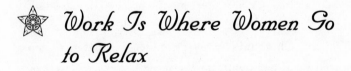

Work Is Where Women Go to Relax

One of the local churches here rotates clever quotes on its billboard. Once the sign read: "The Phrase 'A Working Mother' is Redundant."

I have personally found myself in four different sets of shoes regarding work: a full-time working non-mother (before children), then, a full-time non-working mother, a part-time working mother, and a full-time working mother. Currently, with teenagers, I live in total chaos, working on my computer whenever I can. In looking back, I see so clearly how God arranged the working-outside-the-home/working-inside-the-home circumstances to fit the needs of the whole family. Fortunately, whether we as women are working in or out of the home, God never stops working in us and through us — wherever we are.

Even though I know some stay-at-home dads, the vast majority of women who have children are forced to become experts at "The Great Juggling Act." Where are we needed most? Women live in a triangle of needs: the family's financial needs, the needs of our children, and our personal satisfaction needs. Because financial needs and motherhood needs are strong and immediate, many of us put off personal satisfaction until last. Single moms have it the most difficult because usually there is no choice. They are faced with work on all fronts, unrelenting work.

Winston Churchill's wife, Clemmie, is reputed to have reported what her own tombstone would say: "Here lies a woman who was always tired. She lived in a world where too much was required." For many of us, God alone pulls us through the pleasures/exhaustion of our callings — children, work, or both — as well as our struggles to discern what our callings are.

Joanna related her story: "For five years, I had prayed for a job that would help my family financially. Before children, I'd been a trained professional, but had become weary of that high-pressured world. As the children were getting older, it seemed as if I'd been away too long to jump back into my field. I wasn't ready to clerk at 7-Eleven either. I read the want ads every day for several years, but only a smattering of jobs interested me. I'd even considered moving somewhere where I could find interesting work, creating a long-distance marriage. The clear answer was always 'not now.'

"I began substitute teaching at my children's private school. I loved the atmosphere and loved the kids. After four years of subbing, I was called by the head of school to help out in the office because the administrative assistant was having surgery. I learned more about the computer in those five weeks than I imagined possible. I loved being where the action was. I saw the teachers and the students every day. I was energized!

"While I was in that job, the school advertised for a director of development. I exclaimed,'" Who would ever want *that* job?' And moved on. I saw the ad in the paper the following week and thought, 'Hmmm. You know, I bet I could do that job.' I started sleuthing the back hallways to see who was applying and whether I might, after all, be interested.

49

"The last day of subbing, I turned in my application and resume. Opinions were divided — some thought I was crazy, but my prayer partners and family thought it was a natural progression. I was interviewed and interviewed. I waited and waited. Three months and two weeks before our youngest child went off to college, I was offered the job."

Joanna concluded, "God's timing for sure, not mine!"

Joanna had the patience and wisdom to wait on God. He will usually let us know where He wants us and when, but sometimes it's a major challenge to listen instead of telling Him what we think we need.

God's presence in the workplace was another theme in several stories. Tamara, a college English professor, shared this story: "Several years ago, I pulled one of those challenging remedial sections, a large class scheduled for one of the dead hours of the day: right after lunch. This class was a beaut.

"Half of the eighteen students were single parents. There were several bipolars. Two seventeen-year-olds fell in love and played out that drama for the better part of the semester. Two took incompletes — one to go into drug rehab and another to support his pregnant girlfriend through the eventual loss of their baby.

"Then there were two students in wheelchairs. Tim was able to operate his own motorized chair, but Jenny had no motor control. She couldn't even speak. Tim sat by the door, and every day, Jenny's helper rolled her to the opposite side of the room and gently lifted her tiny body into a desk. Jason often had to move his chair out of the way so she could enter, and I have never seen an action performed with more chivalry and grace.

"Lida was the unwed mother of a beautiful three-month-old baby girl. New to the concept of college, she arrived each day in one state or another of disarray. The house shoes were the worst. But I was there as her English teacher, not her fashion advisor. (Although when she asked me what to wear for a student job interview, I did give her the advice to look around to see what the other students were wearing.)"

Tamara continued, "Who can fail to be humble in such a class? Unconventional. Noisy and sometimes clueless, this troop of developmental students fought the battle with sentences, paragraphs, and, finally, essays. Along the way, they struggled with nouns, agreement, and quotation marks along with unplanned pregnancies, financial crises, and poor self-esteem.

"Tim graduated, became an office manager and married a lovely young woman, also wheelchair-bound. Jim won first place in the state journalism contest. Lida showed up, slender, well-groomed, wearing the right dress. 'Don't you know me? It's Lida.' She had just graduated from nursing school.

"I wish I could say it was the brilliance of their English teacher. However, I'm inclined to say that for a semester, the Holy Spirit visited my class and transformed a roomful of lives."

In hearing Tamara's story, I'm inclined to think that all the Holy Spirit needs is a woman's invitation and her willingness to be an instrument at work, either inside or outside the home.

Lorraine tells the story of a woman who brought healing and reconciliation to a difficult situation at work. Six weeks before, Lorraine had been promoted into a management position. A problem arose between a person in her division and someone in another division, so she called her counterpart in the other division. "What I didn't know is that I stepped right into a problem that had been brewing for a decade. I was greeted with hostility. When I wouldn't back down, the woman on the other end hung up."

Lorraine was angry and hurt. She barely knew the other woman and wondered why she had reacted so strongly. She spoke to the leader of a third division, and he spread the story around the company, making it sound as if the whole thing were Lorraine's fault.

Lorraine continued, "I have to admit that I nursed my grudge against this woman for a month or so. She had made me look bad in a new job and, besides, we were still stuck with the problem. Then one day, out of the blue, I found a home-baked loaf of bread on my desk from her. She was a Christian and was sorry for our rift. Well, my anger melted instantly and I could see my own stiff neck in the situation.

In turn, I gave her a small angel pin. From that day on, we became colleagues in the Spirit as well as colleagues at work. We even managed to chip away at the problem between our divisions. The first step was a dialogue with no past history. As we gained clear communication about the underlying issues, the problem began to be resolved."

God's workplace is any workplace, which means that our workplace is also God's — no matter whether it's inside or outside the home.

 ## A Joyful Noise

The language of music transcends words. We can hear "Amazing Grace" in any language and feel the presence of God. When my family visited the Upper Room in Jerusalem (where Jesus held the Last Supper with His disciples), a choir from France broke out in a familiar hymn, and even in French, I knew Jesus was among us.

Elsie directed the musical *Godspell* one summer at the Vail Community Theater. She planned to cast children for the parts, but because Vail is a ski community, few children were available to participate in the summer. So she cast adults but created a set two and a half times the size of a regular backyard and porch, so that even the Lutheran priest at six-feet five-inches looked dwarfed and child-sized. She made an oversized teeter-totter, a huge tree house, and strung a clothesline across the stage that turned to form a large cross.

Elsie said, "The last night of the show, a cute young couple attended the performance. The wife was very, very pregnant. During the first part of the play, her water broke. Her husband was in a panic to get her to the hospital, but during intermission, she went into the ladies' room and cleaned herself up. She said, 'I have to see the end of this play.' After the play was over, her husband rushed her to the hospital, where she delivered a baby boy.

"The next day, her husband called and told me, 'I wanted to let you know that my wife was so touched and moved by the play that she has named our son Christian.'"

The musical obviously carried a message so important that this woman was more determined to hear the complete story than she was to get to a hospital to give birth. Elsie concluded, "I also felt touched by God through that musical. It turned my belief system around. I stopped trying to control everything, and all the things I'd heard in childhood about God clicked on for me."

Music can go straight to the heart — bypassing arguments of the mind, bypassing painful experience, bypassing the clutter of daily life — to turn lives toward God. Music can also be an arena for disagreement. People have left churches over music, which is why making a joyful noise to God — alone — as the audience is so important. Women as well as men have the opportunity to offer gifts as singers, accompanists, and bridge builders to enhance the Kingdom in an area fraught with emotions — making sure that the soaring joy of the Holy Spirit prevails over petty arguments concerning music.

Rachel tells some stories about her experience as the children's choir coordinator at her church, with over one hundred children from preschool to sixth grade. Working under the music minister, she was responsible for two musicals a year, as well as two weekly services — in the church itself and on the radio. The pastor was a perfectionist who reamed the music minister at the weekly staff meetings about every little thing that went wrong. The music minister then passed on the pressure and criticism to the children's choir director. As a result, Rachel said, "I lost my spirituality working in the church."

She continued, "However, there were some wonderful, sparkling moments when I knew God was using me." She went on to tell about an early service one Palm Sunday, when the doors of the church were open and the children were singing. A homeless person walking by heard the music and felt drawn into the sanctuary. Rachel knew the children's choir had been the vehicle for that lonely person to feel welcomed into the church.

Eventually, she changed jobs and became the music teacher at another denomination's church-related school, where, bit by bit, she felt her spirituality return. When she led the children in certain pieces of music, she experienced the Holy Spirit as a wave sweeping over her, through the children's voices, and out into the whole room.

One of her students was a beautiful, but painfully shy girl. Rachel asked her to sing a solo, coaching her and encouraging her. Several years later, the girl's father came up to Rachel and said, "My daughter is the person she is today because of you. You encouraged her and gave her a poise and confidence she would not have had otherwise." By being faithful to her own gift of music, Rachel was able to help build the Kingdom through song.

A woman named Karla felt convinced that her son needed to be a part of the church's music program. She brought him in and talked with the choir director, explaining that she sensed her child might be afraid to join the choir, but that she had an inner conviction that the music program would enable him to overcome his fears. The choir director trusted the mother's instinct and agreed to give it a try.

Week after week, the boy cried, pulling himself apart from the group, and huddled in a pew. The mother continued to bring him, knowing that sooner or later things would click. Sure enough, little by little, the boy inched closer, finally joining the group and singing with the rest of the children. After a few years, he was offered a major part in the Christmas production, and he stole the show.

In one church, the new minister requested a particular hymn that he loved. Because the choir was unfamiliar with it, they rehearsed it for some time before feeling ready to sing it on Sunday. When the big day arrived and the choir started singing the hymn, they realized that the minister wasn't singing along. To encourage him, one of the choir members leaned over and stage-whispered, "This is your song. Sing out, precious!" What she didn't know is that she had spoken directly into his microphone — so her words rang out, encouraging the whole church to sing. "Sing out, precious!" has become the choir's slogan.

Because music is a special language, women in tune (pun intended!) with God can use it to build the Kingdom in the lives of many people. One woman, a former choir director, retired from her position and decided to rejoin the church choir as a singer. Now that she is back, several of the older parishioners have heard her beautiful soprano voice and asked her if she would sing at their funerals. "I have the clear sense that God is using me again," she said.

 ## Committees and Grace

When I interviewed women and asked for stories of God's grace in their lives, nobody mentioned committee meetings. In fact, I had to beat the bushes for stories of how God worked through church committees. Most of us have experienced committee meetings in one way or another: some tingle with purpose, excitement, and new ideas; others are so tedious that we spend most of the time praying for the meeting to end.

Perhaps because "The Committee" was a male domain for so long, both in church and in the workplace, we women as relative newcomers do not view committee work as opportunities ripe for God's work — at least compared to how He works in other areas of our lives. However, if we believe that God can work through any situation, then He is present in committee work if we open ourselves to the possibility.

Tammie's church was in a slump — the rector had left and the interim was an autocrat; attendance was suffering over the issue of the gay bishop; the youth group wasn't "cool"; and general malaise had taken over. "In my own case, I had a hard time getting up much enthusiasm for more than an occasional Sunday visit, said Tammie. "So when the director of lay ministry called last May and asked if I'd chair the adult education committee, I said okay. And did nothing.

"Then I attended a convention where the speaker was a leader in spiritual formation. Her suggestion for revitalization was to find out where the parish's passion lies. Then, center everything — the hymns, sermons, Sunday schools, study groups, Vacation Bible School — around that subject. I gave this suggestion to the rector, but he seemed pretty blasé. Though I remained remotely interested, again I did nothing.

"Last week, I was moved to attend a "Mission and Outreach Meeting," just to get a grip on what was happening at our church. The attendance was slim — the new deacon and four people besides me. No chair. When the deacon and I talked afterward, we were pretty let down. Between the hodgepodge of people, the lack of information, the missing leadership, and so on, we both felt the meeting was a bust.

"Then it dawned on us. The passion was right under our noses. Hospitality. If I had a nickel for every reception I'd put on — well, with hospitality as a focus, we could move out of the parish hall into the community with energy, then the Spirit could lead us to create the new mission we felt called to establish. Maybe I could even get with the program and create learning environments that support hospitality within the church too."

All it takes is a spark of energy to get the ball rolling again, and in this case the Holy Spirit provided a starting place for re-energizing this church, both within and without. And it was a deadly committee that served as the catalyst!

Susannah's husband had been elected to the vestry of their church right before he went to seminary, and discovered he hated vestry meetings. When he was ordained, the realization hit him full force: the upside of his new calling was having the opportunity to do all the priestly duties he loved, but the downside was facing a lifetime of vestry meetings.

In his first position as solo priest, the vestry meetings were like snake pits. For example, someone attacked the choir director and he stomped out, quitting. All they needed were pies to throw in each others' faces — "and then," said Susannah, "they turned on my husband."

Susannah was furious. She said, "I wanted to go and give that committee a piece of my mind. I decided not a single one of those vestry members had passed Kindergarten 101: How to Get Along with Friends. The hardest thing for me as a new priest's wife was to learn to keep my mouth shut. So instead of getting angry every month, I decided to pray for them. Since then, every time my husband has a vestry meeting, I'm at home praying." Within two years, the vestry had become — well, not exactly a party — but at least a less vituperative and more congenial group.

One of the church committees least fraught with in-fighting is the altar guild, the group responsible for preparing the altar for communion — although it's true that feathers can get ruffled if the altar cloths aren't ironed perfectly or the flowers aren't arranged just so. Things are certainly easier now, when linens, candles, and altar cloths are available through catalogs. A woman named Janene told the story of what women used to do in the days when churches were first established in West Texas. "Being unable to afford expensive fair linen, the altar guild, consisting of three or four dedicated women, procured unused canvas 'logs' from their husbands' offices. They repeatedly boiled, bleached, washed, and ironed this fabric until it became, in their critical judgment, acceptable to God and fit to adorn the altar of the new chapel. They also contributed damask napkins to use on the altar, and found pillows from sparsely furnished bedrooms for the kneelers at the altar rail. Finally, they gathered silver and brass trays to use as collection plates."

With necessity as the mother of invention, these women from the early part of the twentieth century built the Kingdom out in the dust of West Texas by creating a holy altar from the pieces of their lives. In this case, the committee of women made it possible to carry on their church's tradition in an otherwise barren place.

Conducting a committee is a fine art, and if the conductor is a maestro, meetings can result in a symphonic blending of thought, action, and personalities. An essential part of most church structures, committees can be the opportunity for a dogfight (civilized or not) or they can be a venue for God's will to shine through. That's why it's always best to start with a prayer.

Vacation Bible School

Vacation Bible School means different things to different women. For some, it means free babysitting during a hectic summer. For others, it provides an opportunity to spread the Gospel to children in the community. For almost everyone involved, it is — at one point or another — a zoo. Between shipments of the wrong glitter, hurt feelings over who gets to be the storyteller, snacks that run out — it's a wonder that the Gospel gets told. Yet it does, and year after year, children are introduced to the person of Jesus Christ.

Marietta, a woman from California, wrote me with this story. "As the director of Christian formation at our Presbyterian church, I was responsible for getting a person to run our Vacation Bible School. I called a woman on the minister's recommendation and asked her if she would pray about it and call me back. She did. And agreed to head it up that year. We met in my office for an hour and a half and I gave her the material — neatly packaged and organized. I went ahead and did the preparatory things like advertising in the newspaper and making flyers for the bulletin. Six weeks went by, then right before the event, she called and said, 'I can't do it. I've changed my mind. I'm going to Hawaii with my husband.'"

Marietta continued, "This just shows how far I have to go in my spiritual journey, but I was furious. I knew I couldn't recruit anyone to take on such a massive task this late in the game, and I would have to do it myself.

"With teeth clenched, I prayed and then got to work. Not exactly the queen of recruiters in the first place, I must have called every woman in the church to sign up the necessary volunteers, and received responses like, 'I can't; it's not my gift.' "I can't; I'm working.' 'I can't; I'll be out of town." In short, all the usual (and perfectly acceptable) reasons people can't help out. After getting 'phone ear,' I finally filled all the slots, Praise God!

"About a week before VBS started, I couldn't believe it when one of the teachers called and backed out; then, two days before, the snacks lady called and reneged. Scrambling, again with fervent prayer, I found replacements. Sunday morning before the Monday kickoff, I received yet another phone call from the replacement snacks lady. She said, 'I just realized, I can't do it after all.'

"At this point, exhausted and already wearing at least three hats for the event, I broke down in my office crying. 'Oh, Lord,' I begged. 'Please help me! Please send me a snacks lady!' Just then, the choir director walked by. She came into my office, placed her hand on my shoulder, and joined my prayer. Within the hour, I had two snacks ladies, who ended up having a rip-roaring time — relating the snacks to the lesson and showing God's love to each child who walked in the door. Just goes to show you when God's in charge, everything falls into place."

Another woman, Miriam, tells this story of her experience working with Vacation Bible School: "When the director called me to volunteer, I said okay because I had two children who'd be participating that summer, and the year before I'd had to work and couldn't do my share. I got the five-year-old class.

"The training was good and the materials were easy to follow and understand, plus I had two teen helpers, which were all incredible blessings because I had never worked with five-year-olds before. What I didn't know is that three hyperactive kids mixed in among fifteen little ones can present a challenge as great as climbing Mt. Everest. At least for me since I'm used to working with older people."

Miriam laughed. "We got through that week by the grace of God and the expertise of the teen helpers. I might as well have had a huge neon sign blinking on my chest saying, 'Sucker!' I chased those kids around the room like monkeys. I prayed that they'd learn about the love of Jesus — but what I learned was that my gifts lie elsewhere."

One woman volunteered for Vacation Bible School as the art teacher, which meant that she helped the children with crafts for thirty minutes each day. The second day, she was showing some of the little ones how to make and decorate a pennant for being on 'God's Team,' when one small child threw up spectacularly all over everything. The art teacher said, "My mother was my helper, and neither of us does barf well — we're sympathetic gaggers. Fortunately, one of the teenagers took the girl to the bathroom while I called her grandmother to pick her up. The next day, the young man in charge of sports got sick, and I was afraid we were going to have a barf-a-thon that week, but we didn't, by the grace of God."

She concluded, "The funny thing is, it didn't bother the children a bit. They just kept on making pennants for God's team."

Laura had been working with Vacation Bible School for at least a decade in various capacities, including chairing for many years. She told several stories of how the women involved helped build God's Kingdom during that very special annual week. "Bottom line," she said. Just showing up and being there is the most important thing — and letting God use whatever happens to His glory and will.

"One of my first years as a teacher, we didn't have pre-registration, so parents just dropped off their children in a central area and signed them up on the spot. Well, one set of parents dropped off two really young kids and drove away without signing up. At the end of the session, these were the last two kids left. We asked them, 'What are your parents' names?'

"They replied, 'Mommy and Daddy.'

"We asked, 'Where do you live?'

"They said, 'At home.'

"I looked at the other teachers and wondered what to do. If I took these children home with me, there might be kidnapping issues and the church might be sued. Then we started wondering about abandonment issues. What if the parents didn't come back? So we waited, and we waited, and we waited. Finally, three hours later, the parents drove up. We were very, very grateful when we realized they had simply lost track of the time and didn't know what time to pick up their children."

Laura continued, "Another year, we had one of those difficult cases, an 'oddball' child who didn't fit in with the others and drove the teachers to distraction. Finally, on the last day, the teacher didn't know what else to do with the child, so she sent her to me in the VBS office. I didn't know what else to do with her either, except to talk with her until it was time for the parents to come. The interesting thing was that the child saw our conversation as special attention, and kept telling me how nice the teacher had been to her and how much the teacher had loved her. It turned out to be a special time for the child."

Laura had not been trained in early childhood development, but she was able to be a window for God's love to shine on the children she worked with. It doesn't take special expertise, just a willingness to be there.

And the ability to let go and let God handle the unexpected.

 # The Sick Room

Entering a sick room is like entering into a world unto its own. When you are the person in the bed, reality changes, sometimes dramatically. Getting up to get a drink of water becomes a major goal, not an ordinary take-it-for-granted event. Sometimes we feel God has abandoned us in the bed. Other times, we feel God's presence more acutely, as if He is speaking through the illness, reaching us in ways He can't when we are scurrying around with our lists of things to do.

Visiting the sick is a special ministry, not one that everybody is called to. Even though motherhood prepares us for fever, blood, rashes, and disease, taking care of our own sick child doesn't always mean we are comfortable in a hospital room. Fainting at the sight of blood is an indication that perhaps one's ministry lies elsewhere.

Nevertheless, as nurturers, we women are often called on to visit the sick room and to deal with the issues of healing. Is the person going to get well? Will God produce a miracle or will the person die? Is the person afraid? What do we say? Bringing a potted plant to a friend who's had an appendectomy is not the same as serving as a hospice volunteer for someone with a horrific, ravaging disease. Dropping off a pot of soup is different from entering a stranger's hospital room. The sick room is a complicated business, but most of us find ourselves there at one time or another. It's a place where the Holy Spirit works mightily through our sometimes bumbling attempts to bring comfort.

Jean's mother-in-law, Mildred, moved into a nursing home in the same town as Jean and her husband so they could take care of her as she died. At one time, Mildred had been a Christian; Jean knew because she had seen her Bible and read what she'd underlined and written in the margins. However, Mildred had gotten off the track. One weekend after she had settled into the nursing home, Mildred suddenly became a wild woman. She started ripping the curtains off the windows. She threw the radio across the room. Jean and her husband quickly got her to a hospital. In the emergency room, Mildred stopped and stared at a place above the door and asked to empty space, "What are you doing there?" Jean couldn't see anything.

On Monday morning, Jean went to visit the hospital, where she found her mother-in-law strapped into a chair because she had pulled all the tubes out of her body. Her arms bore the bruises. As Jean walked into the room, her mother-in-law looked over her shoulder and screamed, "They're coming for me!" It was clear to Jean that Mildred was seeing visions and was terrified.

Jean sat down and held Mildred's hands, trying to calm her. She prayed for her and told her that she needed to tell them, "Jesus is my Lord!" At the top of her lungs, Mildred shouted, "Jesus is my Lord! Help me, Jesus!" Immediately, she stopped fighting and slumped in her chair. Jean thought she had died, but her body had just relaxed.

For the next few days, Mildred was a different woman. She asked everyone who entered the room if they had been saved. Then, when one of the nurses walked into her room on Wednesday, she said, "I want to go home." The nurse understood what she meant and said, "That's all right." Mildred died in peace.

In another story, Jean went to visit her dying friend Sue in the hospital. She and Sue had supported opposite sides of an important issue. Sue asked Jean why she took the stance she did. Jean told Sue her own story and how she arrived at her views. When she finished, Sue said, "God forgive me. I was wrong." Together they prayed for forgiveness. Not long after that, Sue died.

Healing comes in all shapes and packages. Jean had intended to pray for Sue to be healed miraculously, but both of them received healing of a different kind.

Joanna told this story: "Our daughter decided to be born early. At the local hospital, no one was too alarmed at a baby coming five weeks early. But the lungs weren't working. Since this was twenty-two years ago, the practice of neonatology was new.

"A trained pediatrician told us that night that our daughter would probably die. He said if we were Catholic we should have her baptized. Our charge nurse, a personal friend, had just trained at the regional neonatal unit 350 miles away, and she was more hopeful and helpful.

"Care Flight had been called to lift our baby to that regional center and we had a decision to make. We were Episcopalian, not Catholic, but questioned if we should baptize her. We called our priest, and my husband went home to get the water from the Jordan River brought to us by a loving friend who had just returned from Israel. We'd been planning on a huge — but later — celebration of our baby's life.

"When the time came for her to be whisked away in the helicopter, my husband and I had separately come to the conclusion that baptism (at this point) was a sign of resignation and that we wanted the priest to perform a healing service instead. He was most agreeable.

"The power of the Holy Spirit was so present in that little cubicle, no bigger than a closet — me in my wheel chair, my husband, the trained nurse, the priest, the open isolet our daughter lay on connected to tubes and monitors and wires. There was thankfully no room for the pessimistic doctor.

"Our daughter came home after six weeks in another town, spent two years isolated from germs, and is graduating from college this year."

Joanna's baby was healed and lived for her own baptism, but her story is powerful in another way as well. In secular terms, Joanna's is a "pay it forward" story, but in Christian terms, it is an example of women building the Kingdom. She said: "I couldn't hold my daughter as she lay in the pediatric ICU, and I didn't know what to do with myself. Weary, one day I wandered to the chapel. It was the first time I'd left the unit on my own. As I walked down the hall I could literally feel myself walking a few inches off the floor. I realized that this was a sensation of a mighty amount of prayer lifting up my daughter and me.

70

"I sat down in a pew. The room was white, with white pews and red cushions. Even the altar was painted white with a red altar cloth and a gold cross. I kneeled, I prayed, I cried. I sat staring and wondered where life would take us. Our daughter was still critical — better, but not out of the woods, wired all over, on a ventilator, with two collapsed lungs.

"I glanced at an open Bible on the pew. I picked it up. In 2 Corinthians 1:3–4 I read, "Blessed be God the Father of mercies and God of all comfort, Who comforts us in all our tribulation, that we may be able to comfort those who are in any trouble."

Those words stuck with Joanna for several years. After she had endured a second problem pregnancy with another premature birth, she was led to spend five years helping others through Special Care Infants, a local organization that provided emotional support for families of high-risk babies. She'd been touched in that chapel: "So as the suffering of Christ abound in us, so our consolation also abounds through Christ." Through Christ, she comforted other families walking in the same shoes as she had, bringing Christ into their situations as He had been brought into hers.

Visiting the sick is not for everyone. As with any other gift, it is important to discern whether God is present in our desire to work with sick people. Ruth thought she wanted to volunteer at the hospital, but on her first day she saw a man who died in ICU. "I still remember the yellow face against the sheets. I did some hard praying and decided to reassess the skills I'd been given and the direction of my call. Now I teach Sunday school."

Ruth concluded, "I try to visit my friends when they are sick, but I have to leave visiting strangers to the chaplains. I know it's important, but hospitals are just not my neck of the Kingdom." In her case, Ruth was right. She is now using her gifts as a teacher to further the Kingdom in the way God intended.

Squeamish or not, sooner or later we may find ourselves in a sick room. The good news is that we can bring God with us.

Ordination and Other Calls

Women have been ministers since the beginning, when they arrived at the tomb of Jesus on Easter morning. As the first to see the risen Christ, they were instructed to pass the word to the men. From day one, women were an integral part of the leadership; in fact, Paul addresses several women who were active ministers in the early churches. It's women in the *ordained* ministry that is a relatively new phenomenon.

Twenty-five years ago, when the first women were ordained in the Episcopal Church, I remember talking with one woman who said, "I am glad that I was called to be ordained after I joined a denomination that encourages women in ministry. I am so glad that I didn't have to fight the battle going on for women in the church I grew up in. I'm grateful to others for fighting that fight, but I'm so grateful that I didn't have to do it."

Other women were called to the ordination battle itself and consider themselves as pioneers in the movement. Still others have the battle ahead of them — or are forced to accept the fact that they cannot be ordained in their denomination.

Whether ordained or not, women have more opportunities now than ever before to fulfill their ministries. Ordained women bring to the table not only their training as ministers, but their special gifts as women.

One woman, Lenore, has been ordained for almost twenty years and recalls those early years. Before she became an Episcopal priest, she was in the Methodist church, and her bishop sent her to a small church that had had a woman minister already. Good, she thought. I won't have to break them in.

Wrong. When she arrived, people said, "Oh, no, not another woman." They whined and complained, but she stuck it out for a number of years, quietly going about the business of shepherding the flock. When she moved away, they grieved because they had grown to love her. They had also grown to understand that a woman was as capable as a man in ministering to their needs.

Another woman, Jaye, told the story of her call to ordination. Her children were "fledged and flown" and her parents had gone to their fuller life in faith. Jaye had settled in for what she thought would be a comfortable pre-retirement stretch of work, continuing in her practice as a clinical and consulting psychologist. "I had become active in a mission church and it was exciting to see how a new young Christian community gets started and grows — but my heart was restless." She kept thinking of St. Augustine when he said, "our hearts are restless until they rest in God."

She said, "I thought my heart was resting in God, but clearly God did not agree. Several years passed, and the nudging from both within and without became stronger. I knew that somehow I needed to 'get out of my chair' and serve God from a different viewpoint. With guidance and spiritual direction, I happily followed up on a recommendation to complete a unit of clinical pastoral education, a training course in pastoral care in acute situations — a course that many students of ministry undertake."

Jaye hoped the course would help her discern God's plan. Her supervisor was a Roman Catholic nun: "She was an eye-opener, a transformer who showed grace, power, and humility in her teaching. She changed my life. Sister Mary offered me a position as the first chaplaincy resident for her center. My eyes filled with tears. I said, 'Sister Mary, God has sent me an answer to my prayers.'

"Well, one step led to another, and discernment clarified a call to respond to the church and come to seminary. This summer, I face the awe-some knowledge that I will graduate from divinity school, and the prospect of being ordained a deacon of the church. My learning from all this is: 'Step forward in faith and prayer. God does not call the qualified; God qualifies the called.' Thanks be to God!"

Katherine was ordained as a deacon at Trinity Cathedral when she was seventy years old. She said, "This was the second time that I had walked down that aisle. The first time was in December 1949, and at that time I was three months pregnant with my first child."

The day Katherine was ordained, that child, her daughter, walked down the aisle with her. Katherine said, "She had come from Texas and brought with her my ordinal cross. My nephew bought the cross at Canterbury Cathedral when he was there on a sabbatical for church music composition." Since her ordination at seventy, Katherine has had a ministry of seventeen years, and is still going strong. She said, "Just goes to show you that God is no respecter of age." She worked with a Native American inner city church for four years, became chaplain at a veteran's home, and also served as deacon in several parishes. Her first response to any new challenge is, "Let us pray."

Emily and her husband were both called to the ordained ministry and serve in different churches in the same geographical area. She told the story about a woman with whom she had shared a Kingdom friendship for many years. Her friend had helped Emily through a number of deaths in her church, saying, "It's okay to cry. We're like sponges and when we get soaked full, we need to be squeezed out to help absorb more."

This friend's mother had an ear infection that turned into meningitis. Emily rushed to her side and, as a priest, was able to give her a form of last rites before she died — a powerful moment for all of them. Then she was able to minister to her friend in a particular way. Although she didn't know her friend's mother well, Emily found herself overcome with grief at the funeral, crying until she felt her eyes would fall out. Afterward, she commented to her friend how strange it was that she should have suffered so much grief. Her friend said, "Now it makes sense. I'll tell you, the funeral was the weirdest thing for me. I knew I had to be strong for my dad and was afraid that I was going to fall apart during the funeral. But I didn't. Instead, I felt my grief being literally lifted off of me during the service."

Emily knew that for a short amount of time, she had borne her friend's grief in a Christ-like manner.

Shelly is a social worker married to a minister, and she told the story of a call they received as a husband-wife team. They had lived for twenty-two years in the same town and both their jobs were thriving, although her husband had sent out some feelers to see whether God wanted them to move and seek another call. All the doors closed, so she and her husband decided to dig deeper into their community and buy a home for the first time. They had just found a cute bungalow down the street from the church when some missionary friends in Africa called: "We've put your name into the denomination to replace us when we leave in a few months."

Shelly experienced what she called "glorious terror." She said, "God had to be kidding! Consider moving to Africa? I had said, 'I'll go wherever you want me to go, dear Lord, as long as there is hot running water and flushing toilets.' And I had been the little girl who eagerly read stories of the China Inland Mission. But now?"

Shelly and her husband prayed together, something "that has historically been a challenge for me. Before, I had felt like I was praying with the preacher and not my husband. God only knows what changed — our words, our hearts, our need for His guidance but we prayed intimately and out loud." She felt that God's hand was over both of them as they began to let go of one trapeze and reached for the new one swinging toward them.

As a social worker, Shelly is an equal participant in the call. When they move to Africa, her husband will be partnering as a minister with the indigenous people of Zambia, Malawi, Zimbabwe, Madagascar, and Mozambique, as well as providing pastoral care to the missionaries and directing the program for mission funding. Shelley is not sure what she will be doing, but their church didn't want to send one member of the team out without the other.

Most of us will not be called to Africa, although I have heard more than one story of women called to pick up and serve in faraway places. But we are called. Ordained or not, the still, small voice comes to us in the middle of the whirlwind, calling us to serve God, even if it's no farther away than our own families.

 ## Making a Difference

An early missionary to the Xhosa tribe in Africa stayed two years. He made only one convert, and, discouraged, returned to the Dutch Cape Colony. Yet from among the people who heard him came the first Xhosa Christian prophet, Ntsikana ka Gabha, and a whole community of faith.

Making a difference. Sometimes we are given the gift to see that the Lord has worked through us, but other times we never know, and have to trust that when we get out of bed in the morning and report for service, God will use us as He sees fit, results or not.

Many times women build the Kingdom by taking the behind-the-scenes work, doing unpublicized tasks that end up making all the difference. The only satisfaction is obedience and knowing it was a job well done in God's eyes.

Mary Jo and Amy felt called to organize discussion groups for teen girls with problem pregnancies. Following one session, a frightened girl came up to them. "My name is Mylin," she said and explained how her parents had died and left her homeless. A boy at school had offered to take her in. She accepted his offer, but discovered he lived with his older brother, who was dealing drugs. They both took advantage of her and she became pregnant. She didn't know where to turn or what to do. She had approached a teacher at school, but all the teacher did was to suggest a social worker. Mylin wanted to keep the baby, but knew she couldn't provide for it.

Mary Jo and Amy looked at one another and Amy muttered something about "there are places" — but Mary Jo broke in and exclaimed, "Well, I guess it's time to put our money where our big mouths are." They settled Mylin into Mary Jo's extra bedroom. Amy helped her get a G.E.D. and Mary Jo found her a part-time job until the baby came. They gathered things for the baby and shared babysitting while Mylin began nursing school.

Now Mylin is an R.N., happily married with two little boys — and very thankful to two friends who practiced what they preached. Mary Jo said, "Faith without works ain't worth a hoot and a holler."

Sometimes the difference is in one person's life, and sometimes it is bigger. It's God's business how widespread the effects are. Karen tells a story of how her quiet and simple act led to a Kingdom victory much larger than she expected. "Several years ago, I started listening to Dr. Gene Scott, a teacher of the Bible whose lectures were transmitted via satellite. The church that sponsored him was the Faith Center of Glendale, California. He was most entertaining and an excellent alternative to commercial TV. I learned so much from his lectures that I wanted to make a contribution to his ministry.

"One day, Dr. Scott talked about a problem that the Faith Center was having. The Federal Communications Commission had repeatedly cut off their transmission. Every time the Faith Center was cut off, it had to pay a fine to be reinstated. The FCC used the excuse that the church wouldn't give them access to their members' financial records to obtain names and addresses. The church had been fined $53 million and had filed a lawsuit against the FCC. Dr. Scott said that someone had gotten to the Supreme Court and was working to delay the suit."

Karen continued, "I remembered when my daughter had written to the president and received an answer, so I decided to write to President Reagan. I told him about the Faith Center and their fight with the FCC. I also mentioned the pending suit with the Supreme Court.

"Two weeks later, I was watching the Sunday services on TV. Dr. Scott was speaking from a cathedral in California on this particular Sunday. During his lecture, he asked who out there among his followers was playing 'Esther.' He said that during the preceding week, President Reagan had called him and said, 'Gene, what's your problem about your suit with the Supreme Court?'

"Dr. Scott told the president everything. President Reagan asked what he could do to help in this situation. Dr. Scott just wanted the Supreme Court to review the suit instead of putting it off. President Reagan was as good as his word. The Supreme Court reviewed the suit — and said that the Faith Center would not have to pay the huge fine."

Not expecting any publicity, Karen had felt called to write to the president. Later she found out that it was indeed her letter that had made the difference. Literally millions of viewers benefited from one woman's quiet obedience.

Linda told this story: "Two of the most delightful people I know are sisters from Atlanta. Their ministry at church is powerful and almost invisible, and yet the difference they have made in the lives of the parishioners is mighty. They must have Holy Spirit radar because they know if someone is sick before the minister does, and they have already called or taken food by the time word gets out. Once, they felt called to run by and just check on this one woman and discovered her house in total disarray. They spent thirty-three dollars in quarters at the laundromat, just doing her wash for her. And they never call any attention to themselves."

When asked, the sisters told me their story. One of them had taken early retirement and was enjoying golf and accompanying the other sister on business trips. The other had received word that her company was offering early retirement to management employees, a deal she couldn't refuse.

They bought an RV. However, instead of touring the country as they had planned, they ended up two and a half hours away in the same state, where they found some land and decided to build a new house immediately. One of the sisters got a job in a neighboring town while the other one oversaw the construction of their new home.

Before their home was finished, they started looking for a church home. Drawn to a beautiful church in the area, they attended one Sunday, and found a home immediately at the family service.

Then they decided to attend the early service, the "proper" service. Very few people stayed for coffee and those who did huddled in cliques with those they already knew. Over the course of a year or so, these ladies quadrupled the size of the coffee hour, included the sextons in the conversations, and turned the cool reserve into a hugging, loving group.

They found their ministry niche, too. One of the sisters said, "One night after dinner I fell ill. Sis took me to the ER twice before I was admitted to a room. Our new church had a ministry of hospital visitors who visited us daily. I almost died three times, and had it not been for the support of these visitors and friends from the RV park, I would have been lost.

"The last time I almost died, I had a near-death experience. It was wonderful, not frightening. There was light, calmness, and a sense of peace. During this period I remember saying to our Lord that I was ready if He was calling me. If not, I was willing to go back to work for Him.

"When I gained my strength back, I became a hospital visitor. I learned to pray at bedsides and comfort the sick. Soon Sis retired again and another ministry started, visiting the homebound. It seemed the more we volunteered, the more we wanted to."

Grace, a student at Yale Divinity School, told the story of how a teacher changed the course of her life. "If you look at my life, statistically, there is no way that I should be where I am. I was raised in a home filled with abuse, alcoholism, and divorce. My brother dropped out of school. The turnaround came when I was in eighth grade, after my father committed suicide.

"I had a teacher, Mrs. Rose, who changed everything. She had two favorite phrases, 'beating the odds' and 'making a difference.' She taught me how to use everything life throws at you. You can't change the past, but you can help others."

Grace continued, "I was a scrawny kid, scared, timid. I no longer trusted anybody. Our class at school had been given the motto, 'Would you like fries with that?' because the teachers had given up on us, deciding that we'd never make it higher than flipping burgers. Mrs. Rose turned the class motto back on us, asking us what we thought of it, inspiring us to reach beyond.

"I know it was divine intervention, but she began to focus on me. She took care of me for four years, even though I was only in her class for two years. She paid for my college application. She drove me to visit the school where I was accepted. She changed my whole life. We are still close."

Grace has recognized the gift this woman gave her, and, in turn, goes back to her high school to encourage the students there. She plans to spend her life as a teacher, and making a difference in the lives of other students.

Sometimes making a difference involves a big brass band, but more often than not, it is a whisper in the ear from the Holy Spirit nudging us to do something for someone else, something as simple as washing someone's clothes. We build the Kingdom load by load, phone call by phone call, making a difference in the life of one person at a time.

Who We Are

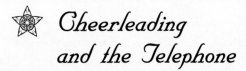

Cheerleading and the Telephone

Whether it's true or not, we women have the reputation of nurturers. One woman said, "I could tell the difference immediately between my son and my daughter. My son was a cuddly baby and loved to be held. So was my daughter, but with a major difference. She had barely grown out of the moto-reflex stage, when I noticed that when I held her and patted her, *she was patting me back*. Six weeks old and she was already nurturing me. This was the little girl who pushed her dollies in the same toy Jeep her brother used for imaginary tank battles. Makes you wonder if some of the nurturing instincts aren't inborn after all."

A woman named Miranda offered these insights: "My story of experiencing the Kingdom of God as a woman, with women, involves a friend in her nineties. She has fostered a devout following in our parish and is known for her gifts of prayer. With her small body, her soft, carefully colored and waved blond hair that framed her face — a face with a beatific smile on it most of the time — she was a reassuring presence. Her manner has a special gentle quality to it, but gentle in her case is not weak."

Miranda went on tell of a particular time when this woman reached out to her. "I was president of a group of women who had gathered together to hear a guest speaker talk on 'The Lord is my Shepherd.' I was feeling shaky. My husband had been experiencing problems with his eyes. After months of testing for possibilities such as brain tumors and other serious problems, there was no diagnosis. Seeing my eyes fill with tears, this woman took my hand and asked me what was wrong. I told her, and she lifted my hand skyward and said, 'Ask the Lord Jesus to hold your hand and comfort you.'

"I was comforted. Being who I am — skittish about sentimentality, about easy answers, and about pat ways — not many people could have said this to me. I knew she meant it. I knew she was looking into my heart. It was a woman's gesture and had an authenticity that calmed me in a way I hadn't experienced for a long time. Twenty years later, the comfort of Jesus I experienced still lingers. I don't think a man could have said the words my friend said to me with the same effect. I would have heard them from a man as a directive, if not a downright silly statement."

Whether we know it or not, whether we want it or not, women seem to possess a gift of being able to comfort each other in special ways. One aspect of giving comfort is to be a cheerleader for our friends. A woman named Cynthia told how a friend encouraged her during a difficult time: "During my divorce, my friends were so sweet and helpful and strong for me. My friend Marjorie especially comes to mind. Almost every day, we would take a two-mile walk; we'd walk and talk, walk and talk. Marjorie was a great listener; she'd offer counsel, and she often included scripture in the conversation to guide or comfort and encourage me.

"She also helped me look at my situation and see how God was involved and how my prayers were being answered. As time passed and new problems would arise, Marjorie would remind me of my past problems and how God had worked them out. In this way, she helped me to develop my own faith history. Sometimes I felt like an Israelite! Just as they had recounted again and again in the Old Testament the saving acts of God in their history, so I would recount God's faithfulness to me. I wasn't nearly as afraid of the future when I recalled how God had helped me through so many problems in the past."

Cynthia concluded, "Even today — many years later and happily married — as I occasionally face uncertainties and feel afraid, I can still hear Marjorie's voice, reminding me of the ways God was actively involved in my life, and I am reassured that He will be active in my life today too."

Since the development of cell phones, our country spends a staggering amount of money on communications. Between paying for local calls, DSL, long-distance land lines, and cell phones, a typical American family forks over around $3,000 — enough to feed a third-world family for a year. Fortunately, God can use anything to work for His good, and the telephone allows us to send comfort and encouragement to each other long distance. These next stories illustrate how the telephone can be a means by which the Holy Spirit travels.

A woman named Elizabeth told the story of Sue. One Sunday, Sue wandered off the streets into the service at a large upscale church. Her mother was a prostitute, and Sue had already borne one child out of wedlock and placed the child for adoption. Sue was lost, anchorless. Someone referred her to the minister and, in turn, his wife, Elizabeth.

Elizabeth said, "During the years that followed, Sue came to church occasionally and we would get phone calls at the house. She had a scary voice; the kids answered the phone, they'd whisper, 'Mom, it's the lady with the funny voice again.' One of us would pick up the phone and talk with her. The unusual thing is that Sue didn't say anything. There would be these long silences, and we would finally ask, 'Are you still there?' She'd be calling from a bus station or some-where and we could hear background noises. But we always sat with her (talking or not) as long as she needed."

Elizabeth continued, "After about five years, we stopped hearing from Sue, and my husband took a different church halfway across the country. When we arrived at the new church, we learned that at the congregational meeting to call us, a beautiful and articulate woman had stood up and testified that she had met us years ago when she was in a dark valley; the phone calls that she had made to our house had saved her life. It was Sue."

Elizabeth went on to say that Sue had changed her name to "Susan." She had contacted her daughter and now worked with other young unwed mothers, convincing them to place their babies for adoption instead of aborting them. "Talk about being made new! God had worked mightily in her life, changing everything, including her name. All those silent phone calls. You just never know."

Apparently God doesn't need words to spread comfort, only a connection.

LeeAnn told another story about the telephone as a conduit of comfort. LeeAnn is a watercolor artist who had been asked to enter a juried show sponsored by a downtown parish. Delighted, LeeAnn felt inspired to paint three new pieces. She said, "I just knew the Holy Spirit was going to reach people through my work."

The week before she took the pieces down to the church, LeeAnn picked up an intestinal bug and lay in her bed, miserable. The phone on the nightstand rang and wearily she answered it. It was the woman who had contacted her from the church about the art show. The woman beat around the bush and LeeAnn listened patiently but thought to herself, "Please hurry."

Lee Ann said, "When she finally got to the point, she told me they had already filled the show and didn't need my work. I was crushed. I lay there in bed, too listless to say anything. Then, here is the weird part. The woman opened up to me about her church and the problems they were having, and how she'd gotten caught in the middle of some really awful politics. I ended up consoling her woman for almost an hour. I finally had to go. I was just too miserable to continue."

LeeAnn concluded, "Taught me an important lesson. Here I thought the Holy Spirit was going to use me through my work. Turns out He had other plans — He wanted me to listen and advise a woman in pain! On the one hand, I'm grateful I could help her, but on the other it would have been more fun to show my pictures. I learned that Jesus uses you for what *He* needs, not for what makes you feel good."

When we take the time to comfort and encourage each other, things always turn out, even if not as we planned. LeeAnn sold two out of the three paintings to people in a neighboring town who felt inspired by them — and who wouldn't have seen them in the show. The third picture, LeeAnn hung in her studio to remind her of how powerful the Holy Spirit's "other plans" can be.

Forgiveness for Dessert

Hanging on to anger can be so, so delicious. Telling and retelling the story of that precious stab wound is lip-smacking, especially when the audience appreciates the pain and adds comments like, "What a witch! I can't believe that happened to you." Many of us women have become specialists at licking the bones at the banquet of our wounds. However, the dessert at the feast is forgiveness.

The Bible tells us that forgiveness is not just a good idea. It is a necessity. The bad news of this arrangement is God cannot forgive us unless we learn to forgive others, which is actually also the good news. Sometimes the only motivation for forgiving a person we feel justified in hating is the horrible thought of being separated from God for eternity. Therefore we forgive.

Being on the receiving end of a grudge brings the point home. It changes everything when someone we love is angry and we are powerless in the face of their fury.

We all know the ins (and outs) of forgiveness. The following stories illustrate the variety of ways God helps us to be the forgiving creatures He wants us to be.

Mary's best friend died in June. They had known each other for thirty years and Mary was devastated at the loss. To her surprise, her friend's husband remarried within three months. How could he treat his wife's memory with such appalling disregard? Mary felt deeply angry and turned down an invitation to visit the husband and his new wife. She hung onto her anger for months. Then Mary's own husband died. She was sitting in church one day when suddenly a wave hit her: for the first time, she understood the depth of loneliness her friend's husband had experienced. In that moment, she was able to forgive him for marrying another woman so quickly. She said, "I'm still not ready to visit them, but I forgive him and I understand why he did what he did."

Sometimes forgiveness happens in a moment; sometimes it happens gradually. Janet tells this story: "I had just finished a hard day cleaning house. The kitchen floor was still wet when my son's eight-year-old friend came running through with muddy feet. The friend stopped when he saw what he had done. 'I'm so sorry, Mrs. Smith.'

" 'That's okay,' I said cheerfully as I re-mopped the places that were muddy."

Janet continued, "A few minutes later, here came my son running through my clean kitchen. I snapped. In an angry voice I yelled, 'Jack, how many times have I told you not to come in this house with mud on your shoes?' I was furious that he would disobey me.

"About a week, later a friend gave me a pamphlet entitled 'Forgiveness Is Divine.' When I read it, I found a story similar to what had happened to me the preceding week. I remembered the anger I had felt when Jack had come in the kitchen with muddy feet and how there was no anger when his friend had done the same thing. The article explained that the reason I had had such different reactions was because I had never really forgiven Jack for the many other times he had brought mud into the house. I saw for the first time how I needed God's help to learn how to truly forgive. Yes, forgiveness is divine!"

Forgiveness is a tricky business. It helps to remember that there is stuff in all our lives that we've done a thousand times, and God forgives us *each time* — He doesn't wait for the buildup.

Forgiving parents and other family members is often an ongoing process. Even if we have forgiven them for painful childhood interactions, we still sometimes suffer from small stiletto wounds slipped in during family time. Traveling home from Christmas vacation often involves recounting (then letting go) the stings that family members managed to get through what we thought were stronger boundaries.

Sometimes we need to forgive ourselves, a spiritual feat just as crucial as forgiving others. Amy tells this story: "It had been one of those days. My boys were two and four, and after three days of rain, we were all going crazy. The final straw was when Charles, my two-year-old, climbed the bookcase in his room and pulled it over on his head. He was screaming along with a chorus from his brother and the dog. I wanted to resign from motherhood.

"I ran to the room, assessed the damage, swooped up Charles, and dashed to the kitchen to wash the gash on his head. 'What were you thinking?!' I asked him. He whimpered. His brother retreated to the corner of the kitchen to watch from a safe distance. 'You boys are driving me crazy!' I yelled as I threw a toy across the room.

"I bandaged Charles's head — no stitches, thank goodness — fixed the boys a snack, put the dog out, started a load of laundry (to get the blood out), and wondered how much permanent damage I'd done to my children's psyches. To be honest, I was acting a lot worse than my two-year-old was.

"I went to bed miserable that night. About two in the morning, I slipped out of bed, carrying my guilt with me to the den. Sitting in the easy chair, I thoughtlessly picked up a bottle of bubbles."

Amy prayed: " 'God, I'm such a miserable excuse for a mother. These boys deserve so much more. I'm angry all the time.' I pulled the wand out of the bottle and blew. A big, perfect bubble ascended toward the ceiling, iridescent and graceful. 'This bubble is your outburst today,' God whispered. I watched the perfect circle float still higher, then pop. It was gone. 'I forgive you.'

" 'Really? It's gone, just like that?' I blew another, this one larger. Slowly, it floated out to the center of the room. 'This is the toy you threw in anger,' He whispered. The bubble seemed suspended in time, hung by an invisible string. Then it too popped."

Amy concluded, "I understood. God's forgiveness was perfect. He wanted me to know that I could take every ugly moment, breathe my sadness and anger into His perfect love, and my sins would be forgiven. I could start over again. I sat in the chair and blew bubbles, feeling a delight and peace I had not known for a long time. God taught me about forgiveness through the simple lesson of bubbles on a bad day."

Winifred told a story about forgiveness and the Holy Spirit — one of the defining moments of her life. Thirteen years ago, her aunt, uncle, and cousin were murdered in their home by two young boys high on homemade speed. The boys had intended to rob them, but found them at home. One of young men attacked her cousin with a tire iron, while the other beat her uncle to death with a cedar post. Her aunt, a stroke victim, sat paralyzed across the room, watching and waiting her turn. After her daughter and her husband fell, the aunt too was clubbed to death by the young man named Bob. The intruders finished the assault by stabbing each victim in the throat eight or nine times.

Later, they claimed the experience was a "thrill."

Bob was given the death penalty, but the other boy received life in prison, with the opportunity for parole in forty years — a sentence that the family thought was a travesty of justice.

For ten years, Winifred carried a burning hatred in her heart. As the time of Bob's execution drew closer, the sheriff brought him back to town for a final hearing. The sheriff reported that he still was not sorry, a statement that poured gasoline on the hate fire in Winifred's heart. January rolled around. As it turned out, Bob's execution was the first one scheduled in Texas for 2003, so all the newspaper reporters gathered at Huntsville.

One of Winifred's sisters who lived in Houston decided to go to represent the family. Their mother left for Mexico. Winifred and her other sister couldn't bring themselves to do anything. The sister from Houston had already felt called to communicate with Bob, to tell him that he was forgiven and that God loved him. Once she got to the prison, she found she was unable to make any contact with him at all.

The morning of the execution, Winifred's husband, a priest, found a visitor in his office, a girl who needed gas money. "My uncle's funeral is tomorrow, and I need some money to get to Huntsville." The husband asked her name, so he could write it out on the gas chit. She had the same last name as Bob; she was Bob's niece. He started to talk with her about the murders, and she said, "Oh, you don't have to give me the money. I'm so sorry."

He said, "No. I want to give you the money. It must be hard for you."

She agreed. "You wouldn't believe how many people shun me because of what Bob did."

Winifred's husband called her and told her the story. He said, "God is working in this situation today."

Winifred replied, "You know, it's the first time any family member has expressed regret."

The dam broke. Winifred drove around town doing necessary errands, but sobbing. All she could think about was Bob as a young child — a cute, unloved little boy who had never had a birthday party, who was hooked on marijuana by the time he was five (five!) years old, who had never known for one minute the kind of joy she had experienced so many times through God's grace.

Bob never had a chance.

Winifred picked up her children from school. They were yammering for snacks and attention, so she fed them but went to her room for a moment of privacy. Still sobbing incoherently, she called the prison. Typical of our day and age, she got a recording and a "new menu." She kept punching buttons for almost twenty minutes, trying to reach the prison chaplain. Finally, at 4:30, the chaplain's assistant answered and she poured out her heart, begging her to get a message to Bob before his execution at 6:00. "Tell him that Jesus loves him and that the family forgives him." She could barely talk, and she was so hot she felt as though her body were on fire.

Winifred didn't know whether Bob would get the message or not, but she experienced a peace that truly passed understanding. At 6:00, she held a private vigil, praying for his soul.

A few hours later, she called her sister on her cell phone. Her sister told her that she couldn't watch as they injected Bob, and so she just sat on the other side of the window praying. Winifred's sister said, "Then, it was the strangest thing. We walked out and the press corps pressed in, asking, 'What do you think of his deathbed statement?'"

Puzzled, her sister had asked the press, "What deathbed statement?" The press then showed her a letter that Bob wrote to the family immediately before his death.

The sister continued, "Here's what the note said" and she read it to Winifred over the phone. She paused. "My question is, how did he know we forgave him? The prison authorities wouldn't let me have any communication with him."

Winifred started to cry again and told her sister about her afternoon spent in the fire of the Holy Spirit and the phone call to Huntsville. They both sobbed from the deepest part of their beings. They knew a little lost boy had finally been saved, right before he went home. Front-page headlines in the San Antonio paper the next morning read, "Murderer Dies Repentant."

Forgiveness isn't merely a theoretical spiritual exercise that's good for us. Sometimes it is a matter of life and death.

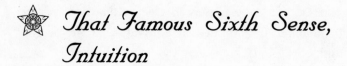 *That Famous Sixth Sense, Intuition*

Women are famous, of course, for our "intuition," that sixth sense that tells us something is going on, even if we can't see it or hear it. The deadly quiet from a toddler's room, the "feel" of a teenager's excuse for being late, the "hunch" that a husband is having a bad day, even when he tries to cover it with cheerfulness. Sometimes this sixth sense occurs out of the blue — a friend is in trouble and we need to drop everything and make a phone call.

One woman said, "I personally have experienced this intuition too many times to call it coincidence. I believe it is the prompting of the Holy Spirit for us to pay attention, to look beyond the obvious. Once I had strapped my daughter into her car seat and started to drive her home. After a few minutes, I noticed she was very quiet. I turned around to find her lips blue and her eyes wide and glassy with terror. I threw the car into park, jerked her out of her seat, and performed the Heimlich maneuver on her. She had choked on a wad of crackers. I could have driven for miles, thinking she'd dozed off when she was choking to death."

Other women told me stories of how the Holy Spirit has worked through their "woman's intuition." Annie related, "Before Christmas, I'd been feeling bad for several weeks — not bad enough to go to the doctor, but draggy and listless. One day, I'd planned to meet my friend Celia at church and we were going to go to lunch with a big group. I didn't show up, and Celia went on with everyone anyway. It was a casual group that met every month, and it was no big deal if people didn't show up. But something nagged at Celia. Everybody else thought I'd just changed my mind, but Celia decided she would drive out and check on me. Another friend, Ruby, came along. When I didn't respond to their knocking, they went to get a neighbor, got in the house somehow, and found me lying in bed, passed out. They rushed me to the hospital. I had complications from pneumonia, and there is no telling if I would have lived or died if Celia and Ruby hadn't just sensed that something was wrong."

Women know that the intuition button isn't "on" all the time, however. I have sometimes slept through a disaster with one child or another, only to find out the next morning what happened — something that could have been averted if I'd been alert. But God can still get through to us, by using someone else.

Kit, a bank executive, had met a woman named Judy at work. One night, Kit had a distinct dream about Judy's father, who told Kit to give a message to Judy. Kit was to tell her that everything was all right. He was happy; he had been reunited with Judy's mother. In the dream, he also said to tell Judy that he'd been trying to get through to her, but that he couldn't because she was too distracted.

Kit is a very practical, no-nonsense woman. When she had the dream, she remembered every detail, but wondered what it meant.

The next day, Judy walked into her office, distraught. She told Kit that she had gone out of town for the week and had arrived home to find her father dead. He had lain outside, frozen, for four days before he was found. She'd been wracked with guilt ever since, and had now come to the bank to clear out his affairs.

Kit listened with wide eyes. She couldn't believe what she was hearing. Suddenly, her dream made perfect sense. Gently, she told Judy what she had dreamed just the night before. Both women felt that the dream, the timing, and the message were more than coincidental. Both felt that they had been in the presence of the Holy Spirit.

Sometimes we experience that inner nudge, but ignore it only to find out later that it was, indeed, the prompting of the Holy Spirit and we have missed an opportunity. The challenge here is not to beat ourselves up. Germaine sensed that she needed to visit her great-uncle in the nursing home, but with two small children and a job, she couldn't find an opportunity for the six-hour round trip. When her great-uncle died, she felt horrible, and her father heaped more guilt on her. She said, "It took many years before I could forgive myself for not visiting him before he died, but I understand something now. God understands what I can't. He redeems everything, even my failure to heed the nudge. In fact, God has given me the wisdom to accept a whole series of possibilities of why I didn't go. Who knows — if I had tossed the kids in the car and driven, we might have had a car wreck and all been killed."

Often when we miss one opportunity, God gives us another chance. Nancy told the story of how she "sensed" that she should go to her father, but she couldn't get away. After all, her father was in no imminent danger and she had too many commitments. Unfortunately, her father died suddenly while spending the night at her uncle's house. Nancy spent a long time in grief over her missed opportunity.

Then, her uncle got cancer and she felt the same nudge to visit him. It was Mother's Day and her mother had recently remarried and wanted Nancy to go out to lunch with her new extended family.

Nancy planned to go out to lunch, then travel to see her uncle. Lunch was delayed and Nancy fidgeted, filled with an urgency she couldn't explain. Nancy told her mother, "I have to go."

Her mother said, "No, no. It's important to me that you meet my new in-laws."

More delays. Nancy repeated, "I have to go."

Her mother replied, "It's Mother's Day and I'm your mother. I need you here."

Finally, Nancy had to leave. When she arrived at her uncle's house, she found her aunt alone with her uncle. They had set up a hospital bed in the sun room, where Uncle Tony slept. His children had all gathered around and had had a good visit, but they had gone by the time Nancy arrived. Tony's dog Chip lay under the bed, refusing to leave his master's side. Nancy entered the room, and gave her aunt a small break to go to the bathroom. As Tony slept, she took his hand, and noticed that it felt cold, but the fan was blowing on it. After a few minutes, Nancy saw that Tony's chest wasn't moving and he had no pulse. When her aunt returned, Nancy could hardly find the words to tell her that her husband was gone. Her aunt had never left his side, and he had died in the brief moment she had stepped away. Nancy held her aunt in that moment and then helped her call family and friends.

Nancy said, "I have never felt closer to God. This time I was obedient to the call. My aunt would have been alone in that moment, and I was able to say goodbye to my uncle. God has a way of bringing things around. You see, my father had died unexpectedly in the same house. This time, I was there."

A final story illustrates that being in tune with the Lord can manifest itself in many ways, including humor. Kristin's mother had worn slacks to work for years so that the Marines in town wouldn't stare at her legs. Gradually, she no longer had any dresses. Returning home for Mother's Day, Kristin bought her mother a tailored dress. It was too long, so she hemmed it to just below the knees. Her mother seemed pleased and said she would wear it to church on Sunday with a pair of blue over-the-knee stockings and blue shoes.

Sunday, Kristin called her mother: "How did it go in your new dress?"

Her mother replied, "I have never been so embarrassed in my life!"

"What?" asked Kristin. What could possibly have happened?

Her mother had been climbing up the steep stairs at the Methodist church that morning and old Mrs. Smith was right behind her on a lower step, obviously looking up her dress. She hissed, "You should be ashamed of yourself in that dress. I can see the tops of your stockings! You go home right now and change into something more appropriate."

Kristin's mother felt terrible. Old Mrs. Smith had ruined her day. Kristin's mother had given her talents, time, and tithes to that church ever since she was a small child of six. The woman who'd embarrassed her was the widow of a prominent and wealthy man in the community.

Kristin was appalled, but tried to console her mother. She said, "Mom, don't worry about it. I know that God has the greatest sense of humor in the universe. One day that old woman will probably drop her drawers right in the middle of the sanctuary!" Her mother laughed.

The next month, Kristin's mother had a different story to tell about church. At eighty-six, Mrs. Smith needed help getting up the aisle to the communion rail. Leaning heavily on two ushers' arms, she approached the front of the church, where she started to kneel. At the same moment, the elastic on her underwear snapped and before she knew what was happening, her panties had slipped to her ankles. Mortified, she began to stomp up and down, trying to disentangle herself from her underwear. The ushers bent down to help her but they only made things worse. In front of the entire congregation, one of the ushers finally extricated her unmentionables and handed them to her. Mrs. Smith threw them in her purse, forgot about her disability, and "flew" down the aisle.

Kristin said, "Praise the Lord! She's been healed!"

Because Kristin is a woman in relationship with God at many levels, her intuition was right on target, proving that "Vengeance is mine, saith the Lord." Nothing her mother could have said or done would have shown up Mrs. Smith's pride better than what happened. The instinct to wait and let God teach the lesson is important.

 # Neighbors and the Welcome Wagon of Life

We all know from the Good Samaritan story that our neighbor is not just the person who lives next door or the friend who thinks, acts, dresses the way we do. Neighbors are all those we meet in the course of our daily lives. The Bible says that mercy is key in neighborliness — mercy to the lovable as well as the unlovable.

For years, I thought that the neighbor in the Good Samaritan was the man attacked by thieves, with the message that we are to be nice to our neighbors — those in trouble. But the neighbor is the Good Samaritan, the one who showed mercy — the unlikely candidate to demonstrate kindness.

The goal of the parable, of course, is to teach that we are to be good neighbors like the Samaritan. The stories in this chapter illustrate the way women build the Kingdom through showing mercy to the people around them — the ones next door as well as the ones on the road to somewhere else.

Loretta had been browsing in a resale shop, looking for fun things to decorate her new office at a local college. She stumbled onto a handmade quilted pillow, with an angel reading a book against the backdrop of a starry night. She had to have that pillow. When she took it up to pay, she started talking with the woman and the conversation quickly turned to faith. The woman told Loretta the story of how her child had died and how the Lord had blessed her in spite of the tragedy. Loretta listened with sympathy and understanding. When the woman was finished, she said, "Here. Don't pay me. I want you to have this pillow." Touched, Loretta thanked her. She propped the pillow up in her office and now when she looks at it, she is reminded of the grace of God and the neighbor she met in a secondhand shop.

Neighbors are everywhere, even in the bed next to you in a nursing home. Jan told this story of how God worked through her and her mother at a care facility. With a job and family, Jan had no leftover energy to take care of her mother's constant needs. She had to put her mother in a nursing home, and she visited her every other day. One day, she learned that the woman in the bed next to her mom had no family and no visitors. Jan began bringing her little things when she came to see her mother.

The lady was so grateful to have someone take an interest in her that she perked up and began to involve herself in activities at the facility. Likewise, Jan's mother also became active in life at the nursing home. She and the lady became great friends and encouragers for each other. Jan began to look around for others with no visitors, to bring them into the group for tea parties and activities they all enjoyed. Neighborliness spread throughout the home.

One of the most remarkable stories I heard was from Rhonda, who acted as a neighbor to — of all people — her husband's ex-wife. When Rhonda first married Harold, his first wife, Diane, was jealous and standoffish. But then Diane married another man (also named Harold), and the two couples began to communicate and spend time together.

It finally hit Diane how devoted Rhonda was to the well-being of everyone in the new family configuration, placing her own needs last in the family dynamics. Rhonda and Diane became close friends. "We even shared shoes," said Rhonda.

Eventually Diane and the second Harold also divorced and Diane found a new boyfriend. After a while, they too broke up, and Rhonda was the one Diane turned to. Rhonda drove three hours to take Diane out to dinner and cheer her up.

Now that's a neighbor. Only God can create a relationship between two women under those conditions.

A story from Shelly illustrates how we are called to be neighbors to people in very different circumstances from ours. Shelly said, "I have worked in the African-American communities of Philadelphia for a number of years. In the beginning, I worried whether I would be perceived as a white, 'do-gooder' housewife from the suburbs.

"For two years, I directed a child care program that included before and after school care and summer day camp. Children were brought from local elementary schools to the agency's campus. One day, I was driving a vanload of very rowdy children and was quite upset with them. When we reached the campus, I told them to go into the chapel and not to sit near each other or talk to anyone. As I tried to calm my emotions, a little first-grade girl asked, 'Ms. Shelly, are you angry with us?'

"I told her that I was angry because of how they were misbehaving but not at them and that I cared about them. She then asked, 'Do you pray for us?' to which I said yes. Then she said something that has deeply affected me to this day. 'Ms. Shelly, I didn't know that white people could care about black people.' "

Shelly concluded, "What had she been taught at only six years old? Today, I am a child therapist working predominantly with minority children in foster care. My greatest hope is that if nothing else, they remember that a white lady cared about them."

A final story involves two literal neighbors, placed by God across the street from each other for a specific reason. When Kylie was a young mother with two children, five and seven, her husband died of cancer. They had arranged for hospice to come into their home to help care for him in his final days, so when he died Kylie knew what she needed to do in that terrible and emotional moment — how to call the right people and gather the family.

Several years later, Kylie moved to a big city; she had remarried and her children were in high school. After a year or so, she discovered that she and Barbara, the woman who lived across the street, had gone to the same high school. In fact, Kylie and Barbara had daughters around the same age. Shortly after the two women had reconnected, Kylie answered her door early one morning, and Barbara stood there, distraught: "My husband died during the night, and I didn't know what to do, so I came to you."

Kylie went back to her house with her and they prayed together. She spent the morning helping Barbara deal with the details of death. That afternoon, Kylie told her daughter what had happened. Her daughter called another friend, and they went across the street to spend the afternoon cleaning the house for Barbara and her children. Kylie had the clear sense that God had placed them together on that street because He knew that she could help Barbara through a difficult time.

Neighbors, like diamonds, are where you find them. And one thing I hope we can all say at the end of the trip is that people will know we cared about them. In the words of the hymn, "They will know we are Christians by our love."

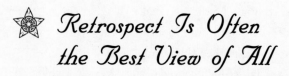

Retrospect Is Often the Best View of All

In the middle of our present muddles, life often seems meaningless. Only when we look back can we see God's hand in circumstances that looked, at the time, chaotic and desperate. As we grow spiritually, we learn to develop this sense of retrospect; even when we are still trapped in chaotic and desperate circumstances, we achieve a measure of peace knowing that God will eventually pull meaning out.

When we are stuck in a situation that feels hopeless, useless, and miserable, it is good to do a quick review and see how God has pulled together seemingly random strands of our lives in the past to accomplish His purposes. Somehow knowing that He has always been with us (and is currently with us even if we don't feel His presence) gives us the courage to continue with the Kingdom task at hand — especially when the task seems impossible.

Mer's story reflects her realization of how God had been working for her whole life to bring her ministry to fulfillment. As she looked back, she recognized God's presence from her earliest memories. She was baptized through the influence of her father's golf partner, an Episcopal priest. During high school, she was active in Young Life and when she married, she and her husband settled in an Episcopal church that his brothers attended.

In college, Mer decided on a family relationships/child development major, sensing that this course of study would enhance both jobs she planned to pursue — a psychologist and a mother. Although she didn't become a psychologist, she sees how God led her down a different, but related path. All of her life experiences brought her to her current ministry, the creation of Wonders & Worries, a nonprofit organization in Austin, Texas, that provides psychosocial support for children, youth, and families impacted by serious illness.

Mer said, "As I look back, I realize it was not just my academic background in child development and counseling that contributed to Wonders & Worries and not just my maternal empathy toward our clients that gives passion to my work. But it is also all the other little parts of my life that now help me in roles I never dreamed I would hold. From being the first pediatric oncology Child Life Specialist to various community volunteer positions that I held, everything I've done has fed into my current work. At age fifty, I marvel at how God has taken all the pieces of my life and pulled them together into a consistent whole, doing far more than I ever thought I could do."

Jonnie told the story of how God planted seeds for several years before she understood the reasons. She said, "I barely remember my enthusiastic response two years ago when my dear friend Cate (my husband's first cousin) asked me to be her children's legal guardian — just in case something happened. Cate's husband had committed suicide two years earlier after plunging his family into financial ruin, and Cate was determined to get her papers and her life in good order. Scott had left that morning for work smiling, excitedly reminding the children about the political returns they would watch together that evening. But it was the police department detective who arrived at their house at seven with the unthinkable news that Scott had killed himself earlier in the day in a hotel room." Jonnie stayed the night with Cate and her children.

Jonnie continued, "Cate pulled herself together as best she could. Described by her doctor as the healthiest forty-five-year-old woman he had ever seen, she swam three miles three times a week at 5:00 before her three children awoke. Then, on Sunday morning, July 17, 2004, after her ritual swim, she noticed that her right side was going numb

114

and asked her oldest child to call an ambulance. Until the paramedics arrived, the flood of normal concerns ensued, 'Did you brush your teeth this morning? Don't forget to turn on the alarm when we leave.' And then just as suddenly as the symptoms appeared, she was silenced. Cate suffered a massive aneurism, due to a congenital defect in her brain stem."

Cate lived for a week, unable to communicate. Doctors said it was a miracle that she had lived past the first four hours of the stroke, but young mothers are the most reluctant to die. Jonnie said, "For that unforgettable, wrenching week, my husband and I wrapped our arms around Cate's children every day, working diligently to build their trust and support. We all told Cate we loved her and not to worry about the children. All the children were able to say good-bye to her, a gift they didn't have with their father. Our own three children were at summer camp, so my husband and I had that time to forge a bond with these three. At the funeral, all six children looked at their new brothers and sisters and wondered what was to unfold.

"As a new family, we entered crisis mode, but we knew the calling was clear and that people were praying. Immediately, the doorbell started ringing and so began the daily meals, phone calls, notes, and invitations from a shocked community."

An immediate problem was where to bunk all the children. Jonnie's family had doubled in size overnight. Jonnie said, "For some reason, seven years earlier when we were remodeling for our new baby, my husband and I felt strongly about adding on two bedrooms and a bathroom. We had thought my older disabled brother would want to move in with us some day. But that space had been empty for seven years waiting to be filled."

During that first summer, a friend offered the family a beach house, and while they were gone, Jonnie's sister-in-law oversaw a massive barn raising, consisting of a volunteer crew of forty to fifty people who moved everything out of the upstairs to make room for three more children. "A construction crew of five men added a few walls and various neighbors and strangers showed up to do whatever was needed. The result in a monumentally short time was that each of the six children returned from the beach and walked into his or her own customized room, painted their favorite color and complete with personal furniture and sentimental items.

"As we move now out of crisis mode, I continue to be amazed by the emerging design. While going through it, I couldn't see anything but the immediate surroundings, but now I marvel at God's view, seeing a carefully sculpted countryside from a thousand feet up. Some of the things God planted can only be seen in retrospect. For example, a week before their mother suffered her stroke, the children had returned from their three-week Christian camp, and all were overflowing with faith and joy and had memorized verses about God's faithfulness. They all seemed to know deeply that they were in God's circle and He was not going to leave them. Their favorite Christian counselors rallied around them for weeks and months, encouraging them and praying with them."

This remarkable woman concluded: "Over the last eight months, my mission has been to assure the 'new ones' that I am here for them and my 'old ones' that I am *still* here for them. I cried daily for the first four months out of fear, fatigue, and wonder, because each day God would show His face through an unexpected kindness. Strangers sent checks, old friends from thirty years ago wrote letters and sent gifts, a sweet friend knitted me a prayer shawl that I wore every day, a delicious meal was delivered daily, and on and on. The emotional work is challenging. All six children have had to grieve for their original families, now lost.

"Yet we are now family and the children refer to each other as 'brothers and sisters.' They are there for each other each day and, oddly enough, each child has a similar age, same sex buddy they are close to. Every day I am filled with wonder at my calling and with this situation, and I understand that my absolute commitment and privilege is to keep my eyes on Christ and not on the rolling waves. He has promised that He will not allow me to fall, and I am so grateful to be a worker in His Kingdom. What a wondrous God we serve!"

Amen.

Angels and Visions

The Bible tells us that angels are creatures of a different order of being, higher than we are in the heavenly hierarchy. God uses them on earth as messengers, guardians, and guides home when we die.

Firmly grounded in the dirt of the earth, I nonetheless have staked my life on the belief that the reality we cannot see, touch, and hear is more real than the reality we experience through the senses alone. Stories from women who've glimpsed angels thrill the soul because it's as if the door to eternity is cracked open for a split second, and we can see a shard of light from the paradise we will inhabit after this life.

A woman named Elizabeth tells this story. Her petite daughter, Sallie, was struggling to give birth. Labor sapped her strength, and Elizabeth begged the doctor for a C-section because her daughter's hipbone structure was so narrow. Elizabeth and her husband James waited in the hallway, to give Sallie and her husband some privacy as the pains came on her.

Elizabeth said, "It was terrible. Then, Sallie's husband staggered out of the room, white as a sheet. He walked over to the water fountain and threw up. James rushed over to embrace him. I asked, 'Did she die?'

"He couldn't answer, and we feared the worst. James just held him. I backed away. I couldn't take in the possibility.

James wouldn't let go of Sallie's husband, but I stood there alone in the hallway. Then suddenly someone embraced me, a really strong embrace. I tried to lift my head up to see who it was, but I couldn't move my head. I was enveloped in this really powerful hug and I heard a voice clearly saying, 'Fear not. Fear not.' Over and over. I don't know how long the three of us stood out there in the hall."

Finally, the doctor came out with a smile. "We're going to give her a C-section. It's going to be all right." Elizabeth said, "When I looked up, no one was there. But I know I was in the presence of an angel. I could feel the arms around me." Minutes later, a healthy baby boy was born.

Mollie told a remarkable story about the presence of angels she herself has never seen. Mollie was a leader in her church and led prayers on Sunday for the Prayer Box. Often, people came up to her afterward and told her that she had prayed out loud exactly what they needed to hear. Mollie also led a prayer/meditation/healing group on Wednesday nights.

Before the Wednesday night group met, Mollie and a friend had their own prayer time. She would do a guided meditation, followed by silence, and each of them felt lifted up in a bubble of light. Afterward, they would compare notes and often discovered that they had each been given pieces of healing techniques, sometimes with startling results when they put the visions together. One Wednesday, Mollie's friend reported that she had seen two angels ten feet tall in blinding white clothes. Mollie thought, "I wish I had angels."

The following Sunday Mollie prayed aloud for the prayers in the Prayer Box. Afterward a man came up to her and said, "You don't know me, but my name is Christopher. I don't usually do this but I was compelled to open my eyes during your prayers. I saw two angels ten feet tall in radiant white clothing. They stood on either side of you and took turns bending down and whispering in your ear."

Mollie said, "I was amazed. Christopher's words explained another phenomenon that I had not been able to understand. On Wednesdays at the end of the meditation group, I would stand behind each person in the circle and pray. I had no idea where the prayers came from, and I would turn my head from side to side — something that puzzled me even as I did it. People would come up to me afterward and say, 'How did you know what you said about me? I've never told anyone.'" She'd had two angels whispering in her ears.

Mollie concluded, "I've had to drop out of the meditation group to start caring for my mother. I miss the spiritual connection, but I know we'll all be there someday. And knowing that angels hover over me has gotten me through some pretty rough times here on earth."

Kathleen told a story of the presence of angels that saved her life, and probably the lives of other girls as well. A young mother, Kathleen rode her bike on a twenty-five-mile course on the weekends when her husband was at home to take care of the children. As usual, one Sunday, she set out and arrived in a small town, where she greeted the group of old men in rocking chairs in front of the country store where she always bought her paper. She then started out on the deserted part of her trip, through the beautiful countryside.

This particular Sunday, she saw a brand-new black truck pass her and then stop. She cycled past and noticed that the driver watched her closely. Then he drove past her again. Just as she was planning to turn off the main farm-to-market road onto a completely deserted road, she heard a chorus of voices saying, "Don't turn. Go back. It's danger." Instead, she turned around and started sprinting on her bike, repeating the passage from Romans 8:28 that popped into her head, "All things work together for good for those that love the Lord," over and over.

The black truck ran her down, catching the handlebars underneath the truck. Kathleen was drawn off the bike to the side of the road — a miracle in itself that she didn't get sucked under the truck. The driver emerged wielding an aluminum baseball bat, his pants unzipped. At six-feet five-inches with cold eyes, he was the personification of evil. All Kathleen could think of was her children and how she didn't want to leave them orphaned. He struck her, but the blow glanced off her helmet. Somehow she grabbed the bat and hit him on the head. Dazed and shocked, he backed off, but came at her again. Kathleen had never hit someone before and couldn't bring herself to hit him again.

He pinned her down on the ground and she went for his eyes with one hand and his private parts with the other. He screamed, incapacitated, and backed off to the other side of the truck. For ten minutes, Kathleen talked to him, asking him why he was doing this. As she tried to get the keys in the ignition of the truck, she told him that she was a wife and mother, that she went to church and that she wanted to help him.

Finally, a truck came along and she leaped into the cab with two stunned strangers, who drove her to the police station in the nearest large town. The man got back in his black truck and sped through the small town where Kathleen had greeted the old men. The men noticed Kathleen's bike wrecked and hanging off his truck. They tried to stop him as he dumped the bike in the town square; then they took down the license plate and called the sheriff. The man was caught. He'd been out of prison a month after serving time for molestation and had been stalking Kathleen.

Kathleen concluded, "The angels were real. If I had turned down that road, I'd probably be dead today, and who knows how many other young women the man would have attacked. Besides, the incident shook my husband so badly that he became baptized and confirmed within the year."

Sometimes angels help us build the Kingdom when we don't have the strength, knowledge, or resources alone.

Visions too are a special phenomenon — messages from God of comfort or challenge or assurance. Patrice tells of a vision she experienced during a difficult time in her life, when her marriage was in bad shape and she had a child in treatment. She stood face-to-face before God and Jesus. They were as real as the kitchen cabinets. Jesus asked her, "What did you do with your life?" Patrice put her hands on her hips and said, "I did pretty darn well considering the people I had to work with. You put so many people in my life who are hard to love, it just isn't fair."

Patrice said, "I was practically stomping my foot, like a two-year-old in my outrage at how badly life was treating me. In the vision, Jesus repeated, 'I'm asking how *you* did with your life. I'll talk to the others later.'

"For the first time, I saw myself as God must see me — whining. Nothing in my circumstances changed immediately, but at that moment, I knew I needed a Lord to help me love others. It's so easy to love people when they love you, and so difficult when they are crabby and mean. God was holding me accountable in the hard times as well as the easy times. He knocked me over the head with accountability: the only way we fail in life is the love we don't give. Jesus is love. It's that simple."

Sometimes we are given clearer sight in a vision, to help us understand something God can't communicate through ordinary eyes.

How We Relate

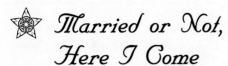

Married or Not, Here I Come

Used to be, women were defined by our married (or unmarried) status. Thank goodness, we have come a long way, baby. Jesus was the first true revolutionary when He treated women and men equally, and Paul was revolutionary when he said that men and women were equal in the Kingdom. Big news back then and, unfortunately, still big news for some parts of the world, where women are treated with the same respect and pride of ownership as cattle.

All of us start out not married; some of us take the plunge; and some of us have gone back and forth a couple of times. Married or not isn't the point in the Kingdom. Sometimes God can use us better if we are unencumbered with families; sometimes He gives us families as a ministry. Being human, we often long for what we don't have. Single people often yearn for the coziness of marriage, and married women often miss the freedom a single person has. The point is to love and serve God in whatever state we're in, believing that He knows what He's doing with our love lives.

Lorraine told the story of how a friend Annette comforted her after a man she'd been dating broke up with her at Christmas. Annette's spiritual upbringing had consisted of a healthy dose of the wrath of God. Accepting Christ was the only alternative to ending up in Hell, and she spent most of her adult life trying to dodge divine crosshairs. Yet God used Annette at a crucial moment in Lorraine's life.

Lorraine said, "The morning that Richard ended our relationship, Annette dropped by unexpectedly. I was doing laundry. I would fold a load, cry until the next load was dry, and then fold again. By mid-morning when she rang my doorbell, my living room was knee-deep in clothes. Even though I answered the door with a smile, my eyes were that perfect combination of bloodshot and puffy that only another woman would recognize as a broken heart.

"Annette searched for the right words to say and came up empty, but, hugging me as she left, she borrowed some: "You're beautiful." I was thunderstruck, unaware until that moment that this rejection might have been a painful assault on my physical beauty. I was alone. Again. And I was unlovely.

"No heart beats this side of Heaven that can answer the sting of rejection honestly. Annette's words came from the heart of a Creator that she barely knows. After the soaring ruggedness of the Himalayas and the breathtaking beauty of the canopy of the rain forest, He stooped to paint the lacy frost on a frozen windowpane. Yet the final brushstroke on the canvas of creation — woman — was inspired from the most dazzling of all splendor, His image."

Lorraine ended with a prayer. "Grant me a thousand heartaches, God, and then a million more, to view my form in the reflection of Your eyes and hear You whisper, again and again, convincingly, 'You are lovely.' "

Something to remember when we dress up, buy makeup and apply perfume trying to impress the male of the species: who needs a man to tell us we are beautiful, when we have the God of the universe?

In the Kingdom, being single has tremendous advantages, for one, the ability to pick up and go where God calls — to be a nurse in the Honduras, an editor with clients across the country, a corporate executive with flexibility to move. One woman said, "I could never have fulfilled my call being married. I couldn't have moved to the city where God wanted me." Bethany's story echoed that sentiment: "I became a Christian during a miserable relationship with a man. After extricating myself, I knew I didn't need to be married to fulfill God's plan for me. Immediately, I was called to a place I never could have gone if I'd been married."

Being a single mother is one of the most difficult callings of all and often requires dependence on God for day-to-day survival. There is no one home to spell single parents. A single mother can't even jog around the block unless she makes special arrangements to have someone to watch the baby.

Kerry told a story that underscores how important other women can be in the lives of single mothers: A Presbyterian minister, Kerry lost her husband when her children were small. She moved to a new city and started working at a large downtown church. The 8:30 service on Sunday mornings quickly became problematic for her children. They were too old for the church's childcare, and too young to be left unsupervised in her office. They were sad, scared, and bewildered by the abrupt changes in their lives.

Kerry said, "One of the pastor's wives, Kathy, became one of my new friends. When she realized my dilemma, she volunteered to keep my children. 'Just drop them off in their jammies on your way to church and I'll feed them breakfast and bring them to Sunday School when we come.'

Kerry continued, "Kathy died an untimely death at age thirty-nine, and I preached at her funeral. I'll never forget the tender and loving care she provided for me during those difficult times."

Being married presents a different set of challenges. It's a good thing "for better or for worse" isn't spelled out during the wedding ceremony (sort of like it's a good thing that kids arrive as babies instead of teenagers). Misty-eyed, we stand in a white princess gown, saying the words "in sickness and in health, for richer or poorer, for better or for worse" without fully understanding that "sick" could mean bedpans or cancer or Alzheimer's; "poorer" could mean no new clothes and an extended diet of hot dogs, ramen, and beans; and "worse" could refer to marital arguments that leave the soul singed and the neighbors talking.

Any long-term marriage involves ups and downs and endurance. So how do we as women pray for our husbands, for our marriages? How do we build the Kingdom within a marriage, a place where God comes first and the Holy Spirit weaves a web of love between husband and wife? And an even more difficult question: how do we discern when a long-term marriage should become a short-term marriage — when abuse gets so bad it threatens to destroy us?

Leigh and her husband had been married a number of years and had grown children. After a seven-year period of drifting apart, barely speaking, being distant but committed, God seemed to make Joel 2:25 come alive like a lifeline, "I will restore to you the years that the locust has eaten."

Leigh and her husband decided to attend a Retrouvaille, a Marriage Encounter–like weekend for married couples, with follow-up programs held for several weeks afterward. During the weekend, several married couples and a priest made presentations that spotlighted special area of marriage. Then the couples reflected, privately and together on the presentations.

Leigh said, "Shortly after these follow-up sessions, I felt like my marriage had been healed, and I praised the Lord, thanking Him for healing my marriage. For the first time in years, I couldn't keep my hands off my husband and the marriage became renewed. I heard God speak in my heart: 'I am restoring. I am restoring.'

Leigh concluded, "In further praying, I came to understand that restoration is a process. The message from God had been in the present progressive tense: 'I am restoring' not 'I have restored.' I am so thankful I'd been led to the verse in Joel. My marriage has not been perfect since the weekend, but during the rough spots, this Biblical passage has increased my faith and has given me the patience and endurance and yes joy, to hang in there with my husband."

Many times the problem with maintaining a healthy marriage is that the stress of work, children, and other activities bleeds the juice right out of the orange. The challenge is discovering creative ways not to let the nutrition escape. Some couples attend Marriage Encounter weekends which provide quality time in a prayerful context. Others make a weekly date with a standing weekly babysitter. One of the ways women can help build the marriage is to make sure that it is full of romance. From planning a surprise getaway to receiving your husband home from work in a feather boa, women are instrumental in marriage maintenance. One woman said, "My husband and I laughed so hard on our first date that I nearly fell off the chair. It was a good sign. We've had other times in our marriage when we have laughed and giggled until we can't breathe. One of my favorite mental images of my husband is what I call his 'deep laugh' face, when his eyes crinkle up and his nose bobs. Sometimes when we're glum, I'll say, 'Remember St. Asaph's at the church retreat?' or 'Remember the mayonnaise incident at the seminary?' Bit by bit we start chuckling. God may be in the details, but for sure He is in the laughter."

Jean told this story about taking that ninth commandment seriously — the importance of always coming clean with your husband. "I told my husband a little white lie to keep the peace. Ha! God caught me red-handed." Jean had a dream in which she tried to climb a ladder reaching from a lake to heaven. An angel kept stopping her and forcing her back down. Finally, a bearded old Man looked down and motioned her up, where they had a conversation. He said, "I want you to pray for Me, but you can't because you told a lie."

Jean said she woke up the next morning and confessed the lie to her husband. He was furious and didn't speak to her for days.

So she prayed and asked what she should do because her apology had not been accepted. That night she dreamed again. This time, she was a child on a tricycle beside a huge airplane. The same old Man as before told her to wait by the plane and he would be right back. As soon as He was gone, she jumped on her tricycle and rode on a path beside a stream until she saw a blue light heading toward her. She picked up her trike and ran through the stream back to the airplane.

The old Man was sitting at the controls, glaring at her. He said, "I'll have to land soon and repair the plane. You were disobedient, but I will fix the plane."

Jean said, "When I woke the next day, my husband had forgotten the whole mess and had forgiven me. I learned sin can keep me from praying, but that God will fix the damage if I repent and ask Him to."

Among women, we all know the jokes about toilet seats left up, television remotes grown to men's palms, sports obsessions gone wild. We also know that men have their own jokes about us — broomsticks for that time of the month and kitchen passes (permission for a boys' night out). Yet we were made to be one flesh, and part of our own wholeness comes out of the challenge to understand and love the other.

How to build a Kingdom marriage is the subject for an entire other book, but I'd like to end with a piece of information my husband read recently — how the DNA from the Y chromosome differs as much from the X chromosome as the DNA difference between humans and chimpanzees.

Astonished, I said to my husband, "So I've been living with an ape all these years. That explains a lot." He laughed. "The reverse is true, as well," I added. "I suppose from your point of view, I'm the ape."

Humor, trust, and prayer — building blocks for a Kingdom marriage.

 *The Fickle Stork*

In spite of Henry the Eighth's six marriages and multiple affairs, scholars have suggested that underneath his furor of sexual activity, he hated women: They alone — out of all the subjects in his kingdom — held power over him. He could not get what he so desperately wanted (a son) without them.

Just as God used Henry's problem with begetting children to create the Anglican church, so God often uses the issue of childbirth to lead us closer to Him. Ideally, the birth of a child is a blessing and a celebration. For example, Katrina fell in love, got married, and had two healthy children, a boy and a girl, delivered on a silver platter, right on schedule. She thanked God with a happy heart and shared her story with other women, praising God for her blessings.

However, in this imperfect world, things often go awry in the area of childbirth. Those who want to get pregnant can't, and those who don't want children get pregnant. I have selected stories to represent each end of the spectrum, all of them illustrating the variety of ways God helps women struggle through whatever situation we find ourselves in.

Several women described their feelings at a surprise pregnancy: anger at having finally settled into a routine of motherhood, only to have to start over; misery of undergoing yet one more bout of morning sickness; anxiety about finances; exhaustion at having to chase after another toddler; the discomfort at having a house suddenly too small. They all asked at one point: "How could God let this happen?"

Aimee, herself the recipient of a belated surprise package, tells this story: "It was July of 2002 and my husband's cousin Mary Sue had just turned forty, thankful that her boys had reached their sophomore and senior years in high school. She was having some gastrointestinal problems that had baffled several doctors. Searching for an answer, she and her husband landed at Scott and White Clinic, and she underwent a battery of tests.

"They were waiting for the results, when the doctor came in with a large grin. 'Congratulations,' he said. 'You're pregnant.'

"Her husband nearly passed out in the chair beside her."

Much as Aimee herself had done, Mary Sue and her husband were forced to adjust to the idea of starting over. They (re)decorated and (re)furnished the nursery. Since her husband was too squeamish to help her with Lamaze classes, Mary Sue asked Aimee to be her coach.

Aimee continued, "I was honored. We drew a few stares — two forty-year-old women joining the class of young couples, carrying our pillows and snacks. But when the moment came, we checked into labor and delivery, and I began my job as her coach.

"Twenty hours later, Mary Sue delivered a son and the doctor allowed her mother to cut the umbilical cord, tears streaming down her face."

Aimee said, "It was a defining moment for me. I could see how God was present in all of the miracles that had brought this new life." Witnessing Mary Sue's birth experience reinforced God's presence in her own.

Most of us can't control the arrival of our children to suit our own needs schedules, but we can allow God's presence in the process, if we let Him enter. Yet questions still pound us as women: where is God, we wonder, in the still-births, the infant deaths, the infertility?

Nothing bonds women faster than sharing birth stories, or infertility stories, adoption stories, and stories of choosing not to have children — sharing, that is, among women in similar circumstances. (Nothing alienates faster than a woman sharing a birth story to a woman deep in the throes of infertility.) In this primal function of women — bearing children — it seems we are driven to share joy, misery, and frustrations with each other. As we bolster and rejoice, we help each other see God's hand, especially when plans go askew.

For example, Louise could not get pregnant. One by one, all her friends had babies. To be nice, she agreed to help give a baby shower to the last holdout. At the shower, one of her pregnant friends sidled up to her and exclaimed, "Isn't this *fun?*" Louise cried for fifteen minutes in the bathroom.

She said, "I suffered — and I mean suffered — for six years. Three surgeries and drugs so strong they made the sidewalk lines jiggle when I walked. I felt God must hate me to deny my prayer. It wasn't like I was asking for something impossible, like winning the lottery. Kids get pregnant every night in the backseat of an old Ford. Why couldn't I?"

Louise continued, "Then we decided to adopt and I found a whole new group of friends who said, 'Just wait. God has something up His sleeve.' Sure enough, He gave us two beautiful babies — the two He meant for us to have all along. I was able to turn around and help other women in despair over infertility."

Women building the Kingdom, phone call by phone call, hug by hug: "I've been there, and, trust me, God loves you and has a plan."

God's grace does not always end in a baby, but always — if we let it (and if we're willing to see the struggle out) — ends in peace. Some women accept their nieces and nephews as their children; others pour themselves into teaching young ones.

Medical science has presented unprecedented opportunities for creating life and, with prayer, God can work through doctors' hands. Although considered controversial by some, even surrogate motherhood (when circumstances are covered in prayer) can produce children who would otherwise not have the chance to know and love God. One woman, an Ob-Gyn, said that she has seen many miracle children born through artificial insemination and through in vitro fertilization. And yet, she has concluded that every birth, even ordinary birth, is a miracle in itself.

Bearing children is a woman-thing, a part of life men can experience only vicariously. In this process fraught with pain of one kind or another, women bear not only children but each other, helping give birth to the potential God has for each of us.

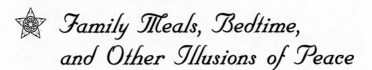 *Family Meals, Bedtime, and Other Illusions of Peace*

Most of us who were children in the fifties internalized a model of how to create a home, a standard of family put together from Sunday School pictures and early television shows. In this illusion of perfection, we insert ourselves as Barbara Billingsly in her apron and our children as Beaver, and we sit around the dinner table and pray, just like in the Norman Rockwell illustrations.

In spite of the release of a new (and more realistic) Beaver movie that includes psychoanalysis for the whole family, as mothers we cling to some hidden and perfect notion of what a family should be. We are dismayed when, instead of resembling a Norman Rockwell painting, our household looks like Jackson Pollock's streaks and splashes.

As Christians, we struggle to lead our children to Jesus, trying to create a sanctuary in the home, a place of love, guidance, discipline — a place where Christ can come and sit at our table. Noble. Holy. And sometimes far from the messy and frantic reality.

139

My husband and I spent most of our children's growing-up years with spaghetti on the walls, trying to keep the kids from bending their heads down and nibbling at their plates during grace. Teaching our children spiritual values was, as my sister said, like teaching them etiquette: (Question: Does anyone know why we have two forks? Answer: one to eat with and one to stab your sister with.)

And the exhaustion. No one told us how tired we'd be from a day spent sorting out high pitched, low-level disputes. One woman reported that she tucked her two-year-old in one night and flopped down beside her. Knowing the importance of ritual and prayer, even though she was numbed by exhaustion, she said, "Okay, let's pray." Her daughter bowed her head. The mother was so tired, she said by rote, "God is great, God is good, let us thank Him for our food." Her daughter looked up startled. "Not food, Mommy. Not food." The woman sighed, thanking God that at least one of them was alert.

Goes to show, the Holy Spirit transcends even the most exhausting home life, if we pray without ceasing. Also goes to show how children will lead the way, as we listen and learn through them. When Christ is present in the home, He often teaches us through our little ones.

Heather's story is a good reminder of how God gives us the strength to carry on when raising children. "I remember the night our first baby arrived home. He slept just fine, but I didn't sleep a wink. My husband and I stood over his crib watching him sleep, and those first few nights, we fought over who was going to give him his bottle.

"Then reality hit, and I've never been so tired for so long in my life. My son was about three weeks old and had colic. He had cried for twenty-four hours straight. I fed him, I bathed him, I changed him, I rocked him, I gave him his drops for gas — nothing stopped the tears. Finally, I simply put him in bed with me and let him cry until he was so exhausted that he finally fell asleep. That day I never even got to take a bath or get out of my pajamas. Prayers for endurance became a mainstay."

Heather continued, "Our second child, a girl, arrived three and a half years later, and the challenge was repeated, only this time, I was chasing an active little boy as well as waking up at night. I had a common cold that lasted for six weeks because I was so exhausted that I couldn't shake it.

"One afternoon, my daughter was howling in my arms, inconsolable. I was in the kitchen trying to prepare a meal, carrying her as she cried. My son came in, frustrated because he wasn't getting any attention, and he started clinging to my legs, screaming and crying as well. I gave up on cooking, sat down, and made room on my lap for both children, trying to comfort them — to no avail. The louder one got, the louder the other screamed.

"Frustrated myself, I finally started crying too. There were the three of us on the kitchen floor bawling our eyes out. I remembered something my mother-in-law told me when she had brought my husband home as an infant and he wouldn't stop crying. As she joined in his tears, it occurred to her, 'One of us has to act like an adult here, and I guess it has to be me.' She was able to stop crying. I remembered her story and realized that, it was pretty clear who had to be the adult in my situation.

"It's only by this kind of on-the-spot prayer that I've been able to raise two children to the age of teenagers. And the prayers have only increased. Now instead of screaming, my children argue with me and as I'm responding, I pray that God will keep my voice even and my responses rational. But I'll never forget that day on the kitchen floor."

Women with small children build the Kingdom, even in the midst of chaos.

Showing the love of Jesus to our children is sometimes difficult considering this fascinating phenomenon: those we love the most are capable of inspiring the deepest anger. Janet's children were in fourth and second grade. She had been arguing with her oldest child, Jack, to go to his piano lesson next door. He refused. She argued some more. He refused. She pushed him out the door and closed it. A few minutes later, Janet's daughter reported, "Mommy, Jack is outside playing on the swings." Janet saw red. She went outside and yanked him into the house, putting him in his room.

She was so angry it scared her.

When her husband came home, she told him the story. "Why couldn't Jack just obey the rules?" When she told her prayer group the story, she augmented it by telling about the rules at their house, justifying her anger at her son's disobedience. One of the group members said quietly, "If I had that many rules, I'd rebel too!"

She went home and made a list of all her rules. She argued with God all day and tried to justify her rules with Him. She couldn't get it off her mind.

That night, she and her husband went to see *Kramer vs. Kramer*, a movie about a couple getting a divorce and fighting over the custody of their little boy. She cried all through the movie. She felt as if she were losing her children without getting a divorce. After the movie, sitting in their car, Janet cried out, "Oh, God, oh, God, what shall I do?"

Her husband said, "Why don't you let me make all decisions about the kids for two weeks?"

Janet agreed. The next day, though, her need to control started to take over. "What have I done?" she asked herself. "My husband doesn't know anything about children!" When her husband came home from work, he asked, "Okay, what needs to happen here with the children?"

Janet said, "They need to have a bath before dinner."

"Great," he replied. He took the children upstairs and Janet listened from below. Instead of hearing the whine of reluctance, she heard bubbles and laughter and happy splashing. The Holy Spirit hit her with full force: she had to get out of the way in order to let God help her raise her children. This insight affected the whole household. Her marriage was renewed, her respect and love for her husband grew, and God answered her prayer in how to raise her children.

Our children continue to teach us and the job of mothering doesn't ever really end, even when our chicks have left the nest and bring back chicks of their own. The relationship with our older children continues to grow and change, and prayer is as essential as when they were toddlers. Once the children are adults, one of the last and most difficult of parenting tasks is to relinquish our agendas for their lives — and our visions for what our relationships with them "ought" to be.

Krista told about how she made the transition with one of her adult children, through the grace of God. "For too many years to count, I have shamed myself for being a 'bad' mother, living in regret for 'missing the mark.' I felt I failed my children by being too young, too impatient, too angry, and too self-centered.

"As the children entered adulthood, I discovered that each had reacted to the same parenting differently. My youngest let me know that I was a 'good' mother. My second and I have worked through our problems and have a mutually forgiving relationship. However, the oldest child seemed to be the most damaged by my shortcomings. For years I walked around with that open wound, always picking at the scab, so it never healed for either of us. This relationship continued to simmer, boil over, and be hurtful.

"I spoke to my spiritual director about the pain it caused. After several years of treading water in that place, a new spiritual director coached me on how to make amends. I had finally arrived at a place in life where it wasn't important to defend my actions any longer. After much prayer, the time presented itself when I could spend time alone with my first child.

"We talked. It is hard to describe the peace I experienced even as I once more heard the reality she has about our relationship. In that brief hour of time, I moved from needing to maintain the status quo to acknowledging that she needed to do whatever it took to protect herself when she is with me. I felt walls beginning to crumble as we were able to talk openly about her pain."

Krista added, "Although I had feared this conversation and my own vulnerability, when the time came, it was really okay. My gauge for forgiveness is laughter. Some of those painful experiences found their way into a healing space — and came out in humor. Although we never have said, 'Let's let this one go and move on' in so many words, our joking lets the other know healing has taken place. The words are playful, the sharp edges are smooth and no longer hurt."

When it comes to families, humor is good. Prayer is good. Letting go and letting God is essential.

145

Who Are Those Teenage Strangers in the House?

Years ago, a woman told me, "I was in the process of raising a sweet precious girl, when one morning, someone else walked down the stairs and started sulking and rolling her eyes at me."

Welcome to the world of teenagers. If we thought prayer was important in raising toddlers, prayer without ceasing is the requirement for getting teens (and ourselves) through those harrowing years as they lurch, wriggle, whine, rebel, and cry their way to adulthood.

In our culture of scary drugs, scary sex, and scary friends, keeping our children alive becomes a priority. These days, bad decisions don't bring merely uncomfortable consequences; the wrong choice can kill with an overdose, or AIDS. As women, we often absorb the blame and guilt for our children's bad choices, and even their accidents: If only we had been better mothers. If only we'd been more strict. If only we'd been more lenient. If only we'd been more watchful. If only we'd been more whatever. During the teenage years we tend to beat ourselves up for our children's mistakes.

A good image for mother/teen relationships is a tug-of-war over a giant mud pit. Teens must gain independence and we must let them go. "Now!" they cry and tug. "Not yet!" we reply and tug back. Because we are older, pre-sumably we have the greater wisdom. However, sometimes teenagers bring out issues that we haven't dealt with from our own teenage years, and the relationship becomes even more complicated.

One woman said, "The hardest thing about the teenage years was grasping the personhood of my children. Just be-cause they came from me, doesn't mean that they are in any way like either my husband or me. They come hardwired as themselves."

Lynette's story underscores the tug of war, the chal-lenge of shaping what's there while recognizing the child as an individual. She said, "In the question of nature ver-sus nurture, the answer is both. My son was determined to get tattoos from the age of twelve. Nobody in our family has tattoos, even though I know it's the rage. I told my son, 'Not until you're eighteen.' I was thinking a small, discreet tattoo might not be so bad and, besides, in the six years between twelve and eighteen, surely he'd change his mind."

Lynette laughed, "By the end of his eighteenth year, he had five huge tattoos. The latest tattoo was the state of Texas on his forearm. One incident helped move me toward ac-ceptance of his tattoos. We were on a family trip to the east coast and went out to eat at a restaurant. We started chatting with the waitress, who commented on our accents. After she left, my son said, 'We must have Texas written all over us.' I looked at his latest tattoo and said, 'Some of us do. Literally." A good laugh helped me realize that this child was not going to be a carbon copy of either me or my husband. God had given us a tulip in a daffodil garden and, as his mother, it is my job to rejoice in his unique personhood. Besides, one of his tattoos is a large cross. What can I say? He carries Jesus around with him wherever he goes."

With teenagers, the lessons abound — for them and for us. Patience and prayer are the keys in Evelyn's story, as she learns to trust that God will help raise her children when what she does seems to fail. A teacher with three teenage boys, Evelyn said, "You know, it's taken me fifty years to learn the things that God has been trying to get me to learn. I don't know why I'm impatient with my teens. I'm praying twenty-four-seven these days. But you know, miracles do happen. Just when you think you're stuck in a zoo on Mars forever, God shows you there is progress.

"Our oldest child, Martin, is almost a senior but he suffers from dyslexia and has hated school every rocky, muddy inch of the road. When he hit ninth grade, he started mouthing off to his teachers. In one particular case, he called his biology instructor a 'witch.' When we found out (and of course we found out. It's a small town — what was he thinking?) we grounded him. He proceeded to mouth off at us and left home. He didn't show up until the next morning. I was a nutcase, but God brought him home safely.

"For three years, he continued to rebel and run away, no matter what we did or said. Now I think we are seeing the light at the end of the tunnel. Recently, his little brother lied to us about where he was going and we couldn't find him for two hours. When Martin called to check in — which he does with amazing regularity now — he volunteered to go driving around town to find his brother. Although I never thought it would happen, Martin had learned his lesson and was now helping to teach his younger brother. The realization for me was that if you pray long and hard enough, God works when you least expect Him to."

Sometimes the going is so rough during these years that teens don't survive. Yet the Holy Spirit can redeem the raw tragedy of a teen's death — the worst thing that a parent is forced to undergo. Belinda tells this story: "It was mid-morning on Good Friday as I prepared to open my café for the lunch crowd. If I hurried, I might get to slip away to church for the service. This would be the first year my son Carter would not be participating in the Stations of the Cross — now seventeen, he and three friends had taken a road trip; they had left on Thursday to return on Saturday. We'd given them money for a motel and lots of advice as they packed the snacks and ice chest. 'Remember,' I said. 'It's a holiday weekend. Wear your seatbelts. Don't drive if you're sleepy.' Carter's friend Ron looked at me with his big brown eyes and answered politely, 'Yes ma'am, Mrs. Wilson.'"

Belinda added, "What we didn't know is that they had changed plans. One boy backed out and another boy replaced him — but hadn't told his parents. So to keep the parents from finding out, the boys had decided to party hardy then come home the next day.

"That Good Friday morning, I remembered the Lord's crucifixion and reflected on Mary's agony as she watched her son die. The phone rang and I answered with my usual business greeting. 'Is this Mrs. Wilson?' asked the voice on the other end.

"I replied, 'Yes.'

"Then the woman proceeded, 'Do you have a son named Carter Wilson?'

"Again, I replied, 'Yes.'

"Silence followed for an eternity and then she continued, 'Mrs. Wilson, your son has been in a serious accident and I am calling from the Del Rio hospital. Can you or another family member come to Del Rio as soon as possible?'

"My heart stopped. I'm sure it did. Did I really just hear that? Was this really happening? As I began to breathe and think again, I managed to ask, 'Is he okay? What are the extent of his injuries?' To my horror, all the woman said was, 'I can't give you any details at this time, Mrs. Wilson, but it is important that you get here as quickly as possible.'

"Del Rio was four hours away. I called my husband, then my best friend. After locking the café and posting a sign saying 'Closed due to family emergency,' I sped home to change vehicles, meet my husband, and leave.

"Within minutes, my friend had called our priest and two other friends. When I drove into my driveway, three women greeted me with open arms, warm hugs, encouragement, and prayer. One girlfriend packed my bags, one took the car to fill with gas, and my closest friend held me close as I cried uncontrollably."

Belinda paused here. "I don't know what I would have done without those friends. But the story goes on and the role played by the women in my life is unbelievable. I don't know how any of us would have gotten through without their prayers and presence."

Belinda took a deep breath, "When we got to Del Rio, we discovered that our son had fallen asleep at the wheel and rolled the car. He and the boy in the front seat were wearing seat belts, but the two in the back were not. One was unhurt. The other, Ron, was brain dead in a coma. My son had broken only a bone, but he had broken much more inside. He was consumed with guilt and anguish.

"For two weeks Ron held on, but it became apparent to his parents that they needed to unhook the life support machines and donate his organs. This is where I need to tell you about how Spirit-filled Ron's mother was. She suffered from multiple sclerosis and was in a wheelchair. Six months earlier, her husband had left her because she could no longer dance and he was tired of taking care of her. Ron's group of friends had started hanging out at her house to cheer her up, so they were all like her sons by the time of the accident.

"When she realized that Ron wasn't going to pull through, she called each of the boys and told them she felt it was time to let him go, but she wanted to know how they felt. They all agreed. In the meantime, she had spoken continually to my son, telling him how much she loved him, trying to help him through his guilt and grief. In the middle of her own grief, she was concerned about Carter!

"The funeral was so huge they had to hold it in an amphitheater. But first, all the students from the high school formed a parade to the funeral, their cars painted with 'We love you, Ron.' The whole town came out.

"In the lead car sat Ron's mother, driven by my son."

Belinda concluded, "Carter was suicidal, but it was Ron's mom who helped him through. Other people helped too; I'm not saying she did it on her own, but she was instrumental. She came to his eighteenth birthday party; she came to his graduation. I think I would have lost my son too if it weren't for her." Belinda paused. "And you know, Ron's mom and Carter continued to be close through the next few years. In fact, Carter was by her side when she died."

During the teenage years, parents and children seem to need God more than ever. Sometimes our teenagers can't hear us or relate to us — they think we are ignorant and embarrassing. Fortunately, our children belong to God and not to us. He helps us all through the tunnel.

The Laps, Love, and Laughter of Grandmothers

I can't wait to be a grandmother.

Grandmothers get to relish the opportunity to rectify the mistakes we made with our kids, as well as the chance to spoil our grandkids. Grandmothers get to give the children back when they start to cry, and the best part (at last) is the chance to see our own children mimicking the things we did, saying the very same words they swore they never would.

Sarah told the beautiful story of how her "Mammy" showed her the love of God. Sarah grew up in an intergenerational household — she was the youngest and Mammy was the oldest. Mammy lived in the back room of the house with a few faded photographs, her radio, and her rocking chair. Her rocking chair was home base. She rocked and crocheted and Sarah sat at her feet with her coloring book and her scissors. They listened to Mammy's radio, settling in for soap operas with names like "Pepper Young's Family" and "Lorenzo Jones." Sarah felt safe and happy with her.

Every month, Manny would study her black-and-white mail order catalog and place an order, always paid for with her pension check. By Christmas, she had neatly wrapped packages for every relative, neighbor, and friend. She saw her meager check as plenty and thanked God for His abundance. Some of Sarah's most treasured memories involve baking with Mammy. Mammy would let Sarah help beat the butter and eggs for birthday cakes, a two-layer white cake with lemon filling and fluffy white icing. Her cakes were like offerings, thanking God for another year in the life of someone she loved.

Sarah did not learn the tragedy of Mammy's life until after Mammy had died. Mammy's husband had been injured in the prime of his life. The family prayed he wouldn't die, and he didn't — but he lived for more than twenty years as a brain-damaged invalid. Mammy cared for him as long as she could. She finally had to commit him to an institution, where he died one Christmas day.

Sarah was angry that she had not been told about her grandfather while Mammy was alive. She experienced profound disbelief: how could God have let something so tragic happen to her Mammy? Sarah said, "I never heard my Mammy complain or criticize. She trusted God completely, believing He would provide for her every need. And she always remembered to thank Him for doing so.

"I don't know how my Mammy escaped bitterness. I only know that because she chose to trust God, she was able to lead me to God. Not with words, but by the way she lived. From her generosity I learned about a generous God that provides for us in abundance. From her faith I learned that I can depend on a loving God no matter what may happen in my life. I don't have to be afraid. She taught me that even when our prayers are not answered in the way we want them to be, God loves us. My Mammy opened the doors to the Kingdom."

Sometimes grandmothers serve God by participating in a second round of mothering. Something may happen to one of our grown children, and we find ourselves in the repeated role of mother. Beatrice said, "I had always wanted three children, I just didn't know I'd be forty-seven years old when that third one arrived. Our oldest daughter started running away from home and causing us all sorts of grief when she was fifteen. No amount of prayers or counseling or medicine or hospitalization or programs or therapy or psychiatrists helped." She became pregnant at seventeen and Beatrice wished her well, but said she wasn't going to raise her baby. Her daughter married the father, and again Beatrice said she wasn't going to raise the baby. "I guess in the back of my mind, I knew who was going to raise this baby."

Her daughter bolted for the first time when Ned was four months old, and he ended up staying with Beatrice off and on until he was four. At that point, Beatrice's daughter finally told her to take Ned for good. Beatrice said, "He was wearing his pajamas when we left our daughter's home. He attended preschool the next morning wearing his beloved yellow galoshes, as he had no other shoes at our house. His preschool teacher said, 'Wow, Ned! I like your shoes!' After a couple of shopping trips, his closet at our house was filled with clothes and shoes."

Beatrice and her husband have had custody of Ned for seven years now. Although she complains about going through fourth grade homework one more time, she really doesn't mind. She said, "I think I was meant to be a mother one more time. I am a daughter of God, a wife, a mother, a sister, a friend, and now a granny. I truly think that maybe the best thing our oldest daughter will have done with her life is to give birth to this little boy."

Just as our children teach us, our grandchildren continue the tradition of instructing us in Kingdom wisdom. Nina tells this story about her grandchild Liam and her mother-in-law, Granny Two. Liam was talking in paragraphs by age two, with a remarkable vocabulary. He corrected Nina when she commented on the lovely flower on the counter: "It's an amaryllis." Living around the corner from Liam, Nina has had a large part in his development through her warm, loving, and creative presence, and she is very proud of her grandson.

Nina said, "To understand this story, you have to know that I am not the bride my mother-in-law would have chosen for her eldest son — she had in mind her friend's beautiful daughter. Even after being family for forty-five years, Granny Two is not nurturing toward me, either physically with hugs or verbally with words, and I still feel unaccepted."

Nina continued. "Last time she came to visit, I arranged for a family meal at a local Italian restaurant with Liam and his dad, to let her get re-acquainted with this intuitive verbal child and to show her what a good grandmother I've been.

"I said, 'Liam, sing the alphabet for Granny Two.' Liam looked at me and barked like a dog, *'Rrrrufff, Rrrrufff!'*

"Not to be outdone, I cajoled him, 'Liam, Granny Two doesn't know that you can sing "Jingle Bells." How about showing her?' I began singing, hoping that he'd join in.

"Again, he answered, *'Rrrrufff, Rrrrufff!'*

"A third attempt produced another bark. Conversation with Granny Two is hard, and I was hoping to be delivered from it by a child performing. That day, Liam had taken on the role of a dog and nothing I was tempting him with was going to change his role. He continued to bark happily, while I backed off with humility and tried to get some adult conversation going."

Nina went home and examined this experience in the light of the Holy Spirit: "What was this ridiculous desire to impress my mother-in-law by getting a two-year-old to perform? I realized that I am still trying to gain her acceptance, all these years later. Why can I not just love her and leave it at that? With God's help, I will eventually climb this hill also."

Nina told her story with wit and wisdom. She prays that her independent grandson will always have the courage to stand up for who he is, especially during the teen years when he will be tempted to conform to the expectations of other people.

Lula told the story of her "adopted" grandmother. "One of my grandmothers died when I was young and the other one wasn't very grandmotherly. So when I got married, I took on Momo, my husband's grandmother, as my own. She was a delight. At eighty, she went on a cruise and wore high heels to the formal dinner even though she had macular degeneration and couldn't see — to say nothing of the roll of the ship. She was a grand lady and most important, she was a woman of God.

"Over the years, she had acquired a cross collection from all over the world — she hadn't bought them; friends had given them to her. So many people loved Momo. Well, after her eyesight started failing, she asked if I would catalog her collection and write up the stories of the people who had given her the crosses."

Lula paused and her eyes filled with tears. "I had the richest experience in the world doing this with Momo. I got to sit with her while she told me all her stories. Then, after I had photographed each cross and written its story, she added a preface of the vision she had had after her son died. She had seen him walking toward a brilliant, giant cross. That Christmas, she sent the booklet out to all her friends. I've always been grateful that I had the opportunity to borrow my husband's grandmother until she died. She was such a blessing."

No doubt about it, grandmothers, borrowed or not, help build the younger generations build the Kingdom in a special way.

 # *Friendships, Kingdom Style*

Kingdom friendships can start anywhere, but they always end up in one place: Heaven. In every way, these friendships are like other ones, except they are eternal. All the ingredients of a good earthly relationship (listening, caring, sensitivity to the other's needs, being present in joy and trouble) are threaded through a Kingdom friendship, along with an extra strand of gold: a shared faith.

When we encounter a Kingdom friend, sooner or later there's a moment of recognition. The Holy Spirit wings a message into our hearts: "Pay attention! This person is one of my children, whom I am sending to you." Something just clicks in the conversation. Kingdom friendships can last a lifetime — or an hour. Or sometimes they last on and off for many years.

When God gives us the gift of a Kingdom friend, He isn't limited by geography. He brings people together wherever they might be. Jackie tells this story: "We had recently arrived in Houston from Great Britain and I was investigating the new post office with my daughters, the youngest (the last of four, so nicknamed 'Me too') and Betty, age five, who thought she had outgrown tagging along with Mommy. Betty had started school full-time in England, only to arrive in America and discover that she had two years to wait for full-time school. In the meantime, she organized everything. At another office, she had every kid in the line playing a game of 'Ring a Ring a Roses,' the British version of 'Ring Around the Rosies.'

"When we had driven into the post office parking lot, I had seen a woman get out of her car with a daughter about my girls' age. She was not flamboyantly dressed like many of the women in this area of Texas. No big hair, no brilliant red lipstick, no designer jeans. I thought, 'I could be friends with her.'

"We didn't exactly wait silently as we were in line — we were much too busy and interested in what was going on around us. Plus, I have a very distinct accent (or rather, I was the only one in the post office who didn't have an Texas accent — I speak English just like the Queen, or so I've been told). Obviously, people noticed us. The lady from the parking lot sent her little girl to ask if we were English. She was also British, and we have been friends ever since."

The basis of this friendship could have ended at their mutual homeland, but it became a Kingdom friendship. "Paula and her husband did not go to church, though her husband came from a very God-dependent family. I like to think that it is partly a result of our friendship that Paula is now an active member of a church."

God is often specific in how He works in Kingdom friendships. Cynthia had attended a women's overnight prayer retreat. Among the list of suggested Bible readings, Psalm 30:11–12 jumped out at her: "You turned my wailing into dancing; / You removed my sackcloth and clothed me with joy, / That my heart may sing to you and not be silent. / O Lord my God, I will give you thanks forever." Cynthia marked the verses with red ink in her Bible and noted on the list of readings, "for Sharon," a former neighbor struggling with the pain of a divorce after thirty-seven years of marriage.

Cynthia said, "When I returned from the retreat, I wrote a note to Sharon, telling her that these verses would be my prayer for her and I hoped that they were encouraging. I also sent her a silver charm of a dancing slipper."

Cynthia explained, "A few months before, a friend of Sharon's had given her a charm bracelet and written letters to Sharon's friends suggesting that they send a special charm to Sharon with a note explaining the significance. (For example, an Eiffel Tower to remind Sharon of a shared trip to Paris or a cross because someone admired Sharon's faith.) This way, whenever Sharon was lonely or sad, she could look at the charm bracelet and be reminded of all the friends who loved her.

"A few days after I sent the note and charm, Sharon called. She thanked me for the gift. Then, with a trembling voice, she went on to say that the very morning of the day my package arrived, she had read a devotional suggesting that she list all of the things that brought her happiness. One of the things she wrote down was dancing because she and her former husband had loved to dance. Then she had drawn a line through the word 'dancing' because it was so painful to think of those memories. She thought she'd never dance again."

Cynthia concluded, "And then the dancing slipper arrived with the words, "You turned my wailing into dancing" — personal words of encouragement for her. We both agreed that the verse was tailor-made for her for that day from our sweet Lord. She thanked me, but I told her the pleasure was mine. I felt like I had gotten to be God's personal messenger!"

Jenny related a special friendship engineered by God for a specific season of her life. "My husband had just been sent to the American Embassy in Paris. Maggie, a gal from Oklahoma, threw a party for his predecessor. When I met her, I was impressed with her life and exuberance. Later, she turned out to be the speaker at an orientation meeting for 300 women. With evangelical fervor, she told us that Jesus was what we needed for culture shock!

"You have to understand that I hadn't been to church in twenty years, but at that point, the Lord reeled me in. Maggie got ahold of me and gathered me under her wing. She invited me to her Bible study, where I gobbled up the

Word like a starving puppy. She taught me to pray and we became prayer partners."

Jenny continued, "After a while, Maggie's husband was transferred to Washington, D.C., and she turned the Bible study over to Elise, a beautiful, gentle woman of God from South Africa. Two years later we returned home to Washington, D.C., and I was crushed. I wasn't ready for the loss of Elise's mothering me in the faith. The Lord must have agreed because within a year, Elise's husband was also transferred to D.C., where Elise and I continued to grow in faith and friendship for another four years!"

Kingdom friendships can start at any age. Lauren told this story: "I remember sitting in the back row of children's chapel, almost old enough to go to the 'big church.' My friend Beth and I wore shiny black patent leather Mary Jane shoes, white socks, and flounces and flounces of petticoats. We giggled and counted the layers of petticoats, having a wonderful time. We were six years old.

"Then my family moved away and Beth and I went through confirmation classes in different states. Years later, we reconnected as college roommates. After we graduated, we shared an apartment and attended a large Episcopal church in Dallas. At that time, we made the decision to go through confirmation classes again, as adults — this time around we were more eager to learn about the faith. It was a special time, that year, and even though I don't see her often, I count Beth as a Kingdom friend."

Kingdom friendships also span the Internet. Naomi told this story. "I had been teaching a Web-based history class for a college in Michigan; my students came from all over the state. One woman, who was a little younger that me, was the most brilliant student I've ever had, and we struck up a correspondence outside of class. As it turns out, she has shared most of my life's experiences (and some are pretty bizarre), and she also shares a faith developed through pain similar to my own."

After about nine months of correspondence, Naomi had the opportunity to meet her new friend in person: "She looked exactly as I had pictured her — tall and beautiful with long, dark hair. It's been a year now since I met her, and she continues to be one of my most treasured friends. I don't know what I'd do if I couldn't email her with the tragedies and triumphs of my life. Whenever I turn on my email and there's a message from her, I read it first. Praise God for the Internet."

A reason, a season, or for life: the wonderful thing about building Kingdom friendships is that they never end.

How We Pray

Answered Prayer

God always answers prayers. When we think He is silent, ignoring our pleas, He is really planning something to be revealed later. "Yes" is the most wished-for response to our prayers, and certainly the most immediately satisfying. "No" is frustrating, leading to questions and doubt and even a feeling of being unloved. "Later" is the response that drives life's planners crazy.

Yes, no, and later. It may not be the answer we want, but He always answers.

Answered prayer is a subject for continued fascination. Why does He say "yes" to a miraculous healing in one case, and for an equally deserving person say, "no," allowing them to die a painful and untimely death? Seeking answers to questions like these leads us down an impossible trail. God's ways are not our ways, pure and simple. Yet, even knowing we can never understand the Mystery of God, there is one prayer He always answers "yes" to, whether we can feel it or not: the prayer for His presence in the middle of the darkness.

Women told me all kinds of stories about prayers answered "no," "yes," and "later"; here are a few of them. Joan said that she'd been working at city hall for eight years when she made a mistake by not posting a certain notice required by law. There were no checks and balances to make sure it was posted and her boss — with whom she had a good working relationship — tried to cover for her. Later, they were both caught and he asked her to lie, but she couldn't. The management punished him for lying, but she appealed her case and won.

Months later, she made the same mistake during a time of stress, but this time she was demoted and had money taken away. Joan said, "At the end of the year, my boss called me in and told me of a job opening in another department *and I better take it.* Since I was six months from being vested in the city's retirement plan, I went. It was the sewer plant."

The surroundings at the sewer plant were bad, but the job allowed her to go to school at night and get a degree as a paralegal. After two years, she was transferred to the water plant, where she met and fell in love with a co-worker. In order to avoid nepotism, she asked for a transfer and, without consultation, was thrown into a job far below her skills.

Six months later, she was happily married and had stumbled on a new and wonderful job. Joan said, "I am now working for a Christian, family-oriented firm where I am appreciated and respected. Looking back at the events in my life and all the unsuccessful interviews, I realize that God had a plan so that I would end up with the love of my life and the dream job of a lifetime."

Sometimes "yes," sometimes "no," and sometimes "later."

Roseann told the story of how God answered a very specific prayer — with the speed of light. She and her sister had bought a red Persian show cat named Bomber for $2,500.

When the cat arrived by air, he had only one testicle and his kneecaps were behind his knees instead of in the front. But Roseann fell instantly in love with his beautiful face and personality. Bomber went through two separate operations (at $1,600 each) to repair his legs, and he was neutered. Roseann and her sister proceeded to show him in premiership competition and he won grand champion all over the country. Bomber died after eighteen years and Roseann was heartbroken. She and her sister left for a week because she couldn't bear the empty house. Finally, they returned home and began to plan for another cat. On Monday, they went out to lunch with a priest from church, a fellow animal lover, and a good friend. Roseann said, "I don't want just any cat. I want a male red Persian." That was her prayer, even though she knew this kind of cat was extremely rare.

The next morning at Bible study with the same priest, the youth director came in, dismayed. Apparently, someone had left a cat in terrible shape outside the youth room. The priest went to take a look. When she came back in, she said, "Well I see that the suckers are still here," referring to Roseann and her sister, who were known for rescuing animals in trouble.

It was a male red Persian.

When God answers prayers, both the timing and the shape of the answer can be unexpected. Lois had prayed for a child for almost eight years. Three surgeries and massive drug doses later, still no child. She and her husband had gone through almost all the hoops with an adoption agency and were waiting for final approval — which usually meant another wait of one to two years.

As they began their wait, Lois and her husband had gone on a retreat, and a healing service was offered. Lois had been to countless healing services and thought she would pass on this one, but found herself burning with a hot flash so intense it made her miserable. "I knew I had to go up for healing. Only this time, I felt on fire to pray for the birth mother of the child we were trying to adopt. I was confused, but obeyed the promptings because they were so strong that I couldn't ignore them."

Within a few days, Lois's son was born and she and her husband picked up their tiny infant — a year or two before they expected his arrival. "What a bells-and-whistles answer to prayer! The timing was a miracle. And our son was the most precious child I'd ever laid my eyes on."

Some prayers are answered with bells and whistles; others are answered with a whisper. A long time ago, I knew a woman who had lost her brother suddenly in an accident. She grieved for months and months. Then, one day, she woke up and was at peace. God had quietly answered her prayer from one day to the next.

Joan had a similar experience. She said, "I had been struggling emotionally with being divorced after twenty-three years of marriage and I often prayed that God would either bring someone into my life or give me peace. He gave me peace. It was awesome. And it was just one day I woke up and was at peace. I can't even remember what day. I was so content and better prepared for any future new relationship."

If God counts the hairs on our head and treasures each of the sparrows, then we can rest assured that He will listen to us, whether we pray for something so monumental as a child, or more everyday things. One woman from Trinidad told this story to her daughter-in-law, Joyce: she kept forgetting the toast. She would leave the bread under the broiler and before she knew it, she had burned the toast, morning after morning. She told Joyce that she now had a little talk with God each morning and she would ask that He let her get to the toast before it burned. Ever since, she's been able to remember on time.

This story so influenced Joyce that she recalled it when she lost a special-ordered pair of socks for deer hunting. She turned her house upside down looking for those socks. Months passed, and all she could think about was the money she had wasted. Then she decided to ask God to help her find the missing socks. "Lo and behold, one day as I walked beside our old barn, a place I traveled many, many times, there in a clump of grass lay my socks. I have no doubt this was the power of prayer and, no matter what, we can come to God in prayer, even for a pair of socks or unburned toast."

Maybe yes. Maybe no. Maybe later. Big things. Little things. The point is to keep the conversation going.

Calling on God in Unlikely Places

If Paul says we are to pray without ceasing, then any place can become a prayer closet — a car, a PTO meeting, a bathroom, a driver's safety classroom, the grocery store, you name it. One woman told me she talks to Jesus as she drives, picturing Him in the passenger seat of her car. Another woman imagines her prayers like helium balloons floating toward Heaven filled with the hot air of her daily requests. Although God doesn't force us to communicate with Him, He is like cellular service with no blackout spots — always there when we initiate a conversation.

Loretta told me about three unusual places and times when she's found herself praying: "I always prayed when my children were throwing up. I'd be with them in the bathroom praying that they wouldn't choke. We had a friend who died choking like that, so I always prayed when they were sick. And once, my son got sick in the car in the middle of the busiest intersection in town and I was trying to hold a plastic bucket under him and not have a wreck. That time, I was praying for all kinds of things. We made it safely to the side of the road and he didn't choke."

Loretta continued. "I used to have cramps so bad they were like labor pains. Once I found myself cramping and praying on the bathroom floor of a public restroom. Another time, I had a miscarriage at a party. I was about two weeks late and just thought it was a bad case of cramps with a lot of blood, so I took two aspirin and sat down. It was really grim, but I got through it. It's amazing what prayer and deep breaths can do."

Loretta paused. "One last story. Our family had to get to another part of the state quickly and the usual methods of transportation would have been too slow. A pilot we knew offered to take us in his private six-seater plane. The trip there with both the pilot and a copilot was great. The trip back, though, was an event of unceasing prayer. It wasn't that the pilot wasn't trustworthy, although he was by himself this time. And it wasn't that the weather wasn't fine. The terrifying thing was that the pilot asked my son (age twelve) if he wanted to be the copilot. You have to understand that the most complicated piece of machinery my son had ever driven was his bicycle.

"I'll be darned, but my son flew that airplane the whole trip, except for takeoff and landing. I prayed the whole time, and I just know we were lifted on angels' wings."

Sports offers another arena for prayer. Wendy played tennis with some ladies who were competitive but also nice. Her group traveled for regional competition, unfortunately running into women for whom winning was more important than sportsmanship. Wendy related: "One woman on another team was particularly obnoxious. She made catty comments on her opponents' shots. She put down her partner. She talked nonstop when changing sides. Nobody on my team wanted to play against her, but it seemed like my partner, Jenny, and I always got stuck with her.

"Sure enough, Jenny and I drew her in the second round of a tournament. We just looked at each other and sighed. After the first set, I went to the drinking fountain and told Jenny, 'The Holy Spirit is not getting through. I'm praying so hard, but my teeth are grinding and I'm ready to aim my racket at the back of her head.'

"Jenny laughed in her wonderful way. She said, 'Just remember, this tennis match will be over in thirty minutes, but we have the rest of eternity to live in the Kingdom. Dear Jesus, help us to get back out there and bless her socks off.'"

Wendy concluded, "I returned to the court refreshed and managed to say, 'Good shot' every time she hit one. Now, months later, I can't remember the score. I can't even remember who won the match. But I'll always remember Jenny's encouragement and her reminder of what's important in the long run."

Lou had another story about spontaneous prayer: "When my husband, a pastor, was called to a new church, two women came up and asked me to join the Bobettes for dinner.

"'Bobettes?' I asked.

" 'It's a long story,' they giggled. 'Basically, it's the women on or related to members of the search committee. We adopted the name after an especially memorable trip to visit a potential pastor. Anyway, we go to Chili's once a month and, well, they usually put us in the back because we laugh so much.' "

Lou continued, "Sure enough, during what turned out to be a difficult transition, I could count on laughing until my sides hurt once a month.

"One evening as we were leaving Chili's, Nancy asked us to pray for her because she had developed shingles. Right there on the sidewalk, all five of us stopped next to a bench and a potted cactus and put our hands on her, praying for healing. It wasn't long or dramatic, but there we were, outside a public restaurant for all the world to see.

"What was interesting were the comments passersby made. When we broke up, people said, 'It's wonderful to see you all praying for each other.' I loved it. We were all Episcopalians, and Episcopalians aren't supposed to do that sort of thing."

Prayer while shopping is apparently a biggie. I don't know whether men ever find themselves in desperate straits in a large store, with sore feet and a deadline, but we women do. One woman said, "It was Christmas Eve and my son's big wish was for a bomber jacket. I had literally searched every store in town over the last several days, and had decided to make one last trip to Wal-mart. I'd checked there first but none of their jackets were in his size. Something compelled me to look one more time. Walking through the boys' section I prayed, 'Oh, Lord, please let me have a miracle. I know it's a small thing, but I'm so tired, and my son will be so disappointed.'

"As I got closer, I'll be darned if there wasn't a bomber jacket, just like the one he wanted *in his size,* hanging on display. Maybe someone had returned it for some reason. All I knew was that God had sent that bomber jacket to my son."

Another woman reported that she and her daughter had bought the wrong dress for an important party. Most women know what it's like to walk into a party in the wrong outfit, and it takes a spiritually mature woman to shrug it off. This was a young girl, still a teenager, and a great deal was at stake. Her mother was a minister, trying to find the right balance between earthly things like clothes and teaching her daughter that her worth didn't come from what she wore. In the meantime, it was Sunday afternoon after a long morning at work, and her mother was worn out.

There was no little black dress in the entire mall. So she and her daughter prayed. Sure enough, in the last department store, they saw it — and it fit like a dream. The mother started crying in the dressing room. When the girl asked why she was crying, the mom said, "Jesus loves us *so* much."

Men might not understand the power of stories like this, but women seem to have a keen sense that God's presence is in everything from the big things like job decisions to the details of life like bomber jackets and black dresses. We often find ourselves praying in stores, not only for the item itself, but also because we are so exhausted from the many demands on our lives, and it is comforting to know that Jesus is with us as we trudge through long days in our high heels.

I don't know for sure, but I'll bet one place men do pray is on the golf course. Maddie tells the story of her golf prayers: "A friend asked me to join a weekly foursome with two women that I barely knew, but who seemed nice the few times I'd met them. I agreed. I can't get enough of golf, and they played at a good time for me. Anyway, one of the women, Gayle, was tall, slim, and obnoxious. Worse, she was a terrible golfer.

"I hate to admit this, but my reaction over the next several months showed in my golf game. It was as if I couldn't tune her out — either her chatter or her presence. So I started praying, 'Lord, help me to love this woman. Give me the strength to focus on golf and not on my feelings about her.' Every week I prayed the whole length of the nine holes.

"The funny thing is that off the course, she was fine. I ran into her around town and she was always gracious and sweet. But on the course, it was like her personality changed and I couldn't stop being bugged by her. Finally, after months of prayer, my golf game felt jinxed and I couldn't overcome my feelings. I also couldn't understand why God wasn't changing my heart. So I found another foursome."

Maddie concluded, "God didn't change my heart on the golf course. It was like Paul's prayer about the thorn in the flesh. Sometimes God doesn't give us what we ask for. But in a way, he answered the prayer underneath my prayer. I really needed to be out of that relationship, so he gave me another gift. Now when I see Gayle, I no longer have those feelings. She has continued to be sweet and I return her goodwill. I also have a new group of golfers." Maddie laughed. "And when you think about it, I learned something else: spending most of my golf time praying instead of being focused only on golf can't be a bad thing!"

Spontaneous prayer is not always answered yes or answered instantly. But it's always answered with the presence of God.

✦ When Two or More Are Gathered in His Name

Strength in numbers. Wisdom beyond a narrow view. Comfort like a blanket in the cold. Spiritual food when starving. Endorphins from laughing. A safety net of prayer. Sometimes, just pure dee fun.

The women in our prayer groups often become our clos-est friends because they share so many aspects of our lives. We have carpool friends, soccer mom friends, work friends, and so on, but our prayer group friends often share all of the above through our stories, plus they share the deepest part of us in Christ through prayer. Women have told me all kinds of stories about prayer groups, and I'm including a spectrum of what they're all about.

Jean's pregnant daughter informed her that she was going to have an abortion that day. No amount of discus-sion or prayer would dissuade her from her path. Deeply upset, Jean went to her prayer group that same day, but couldn't talk about it to her friends because she felt it was too personal and revealing. So during the prayer time, she prayed quietly under her breath.

The woman sitting next to her called her later that day. She said, "Do you always pray in French?"

Jean replied, "No. I don't even know French."

The woman answered, "I could hear you praying in French, using male grammar, and you said, 'Thank you, Father, for the gift of life. I am coming to be with you now.' Later Jean asked God if this prayer was her grandson's. He replied, "His name is David and you will know him."

Stunned, Jean understood her prayer. She had inter-ceded for the baby whose soul was winging its way to heaven while her daughter underwent the abortion. Jean would know David in heaven. As a result of this experience,

Jean felt called to start working at the Crisis Pregnancy Center, where she has told her story many times, and through it, saved the lives of many unborn children.

Jean continued, "There's more to the story. Things were not easy for my daughter. I'm not sure she was able to come to terms with what she had done. Some time later, my daughter came to me in the night. She had been hearing voices telling her to kill me and to kill herself. I comforted her and told her the story of the day she had her abortion. She started crying, and expressed how much she wanted to see her son in heaven. I told her, 'Then you're going to have to give your life to Jesus.'"

The magnificence of God's redemption radiates through this story. Little David, the child who never made it to birth, brought his mother to the Kingdom through two women in a prayer group, and all of them will meet up later in a place too splendid to envision.

The Episcopal church offers a prayer order for women called Daughters of the King, whose primary function is to pray for the parish, its clergy, and its members. We call the Daughters our "prayer warriors." They meet monthly and hold retreats during Lent and Advent — knowing that they are praying when you're in the hospital provides a source of comfort as warm as a bonfire.

Wanda, a new priest's wife from a small town in the Midwest, told the story of Laverne — a veteran recruiter from many years as a Sunday school director. Laverne called

Wanda and invited her to join the Daughters of the King, saying, "We're starting up a new chapter and we need you to join. If you do, we'll have enough women on board to get this thing off the ground." She knew Wanda had been a member of the D.O.K. at her previous church.

Wanda hesitated. It didn't feel right. The meetings were held during precious family time and, frankly, she didn't feel called. There was a void where there should have been a tug.

While Laverne gave her a convincing argument, Wanda still didn't feel called. Finally, she said, "Laverne, I'll pray about it and you pray about it, too. I'll call you back tomorrow."

Wanda prayed about it and again didn't feel called. Still, she dreaded phoning Laverne with her answer. To her surprise, Laverne called her early the next morning. "You know what?" said Laverne. "I prayed on your behalf last night and the answer was very clear. You are not to join. You were right."

When she related the story, Wanda added, "I was impressed by Laverne's spiritual ability to discern something she didn't want to hear." She laughed, "And, of course, because the Holy Spirit is in charge, the group is going great guns."

Many of us are so used to thinking of prayer as talking to God that we forget that the conversation is a two-way street. Listening to His reply is just as important. The problem comes when we have to make a choice. We want to do

God's will but we don't seem to know what that is. The problem also comes when God is silent. I've always favored postcards, myself, wishing God would just send one from Heaven and write His instructions on the back. Another friend said, no, she would prefer a blinking neon sign.

At any rate, we are stuck here on earth with only five senses (and an occasional sixth, intuitive sense) to help us stumble down the path of God's will, trying to figure out what He wants.

Speaking from personal experience, I've discovered that finding our particular niche in the Kingdom can sometimes take a while, like a couple of decades. We're given a variety of tasks to do along the way, but that raison d'être, the deep, underlying reason God created us and put us on earth, eludes us. After years of trying to find the right way to express herself artistically, one woman discovered working in clay. She said, "Yes! This is what I was meant to do!"

Lisa tells her story, expressing her conversion and her call as an "amazing technicolor bus ride." Now a grandmother with a stable and blessed life, Lisa had perfect attendance at her childhood Sunday school, but didn't become a true Christian until twenty-one years ago. Her conversion was born out of the dark pit of failure and wrong choices, a "mirey clay" period. When she gave her life to Jesus Christ, she was so charged up, she wanted to go out and give her testimony to the "waiting throngs." She remembers praying,

"Okay, Lord, bring on the buses! I'm ready to speak to audiences everywhere about You and me!"

Lisa said, "And He did bring on the buses, but put me on the very back of the bus! Being a forefront person before my conversion, I confess no love for the backseat position, even with a converted heart. I have told Him about this numerous times over the years and He has loved me too much to turn me loose."

Lisa commented on her twenty-year, loving backseat training. "I found myself identifying with Jeremiah when he asked God if He were a deceptive brook, running full at times and bone dry at times. For all these years, God has been faithful in meeting my needs with love pats and discipline alike, as I struggled to work, raise my children as a single mom, rebuild the pit I'd dug for myself and make true friends on the journey.

"I have matured as God's woman and yet one particular prayer has neither materialized nor disappeared, and that is to know beyond a shadow of a doubt what my particular gift is in His body — where I fit into the church. Where will I find that magnificent flow of the right-now movement of the Holy Spirit, and know at that moment I am with Him in it?

"I'd been a part of a praise team and have even been gifted with composing a couple of songs. But those doors seemed to be slowly, steadily closing. I still longed to know 'where I fit.' This desire has created a hole in my fabric that has made church and worship lonely times instead of times of community and belonging."

Lisa continued, "Jesus surprised me in October of this year. Our church hosted a conference on the authority of Scripture and our praise team offered the music. During preparations, we had been doing intercessory prayer constantly, but I hadn't signed up for the conference intercession team because the meetings took place during work hours. Then I decided to stay a moment with the intercessory prayer team on the first morning, and ended up staying for two days! I had found the 'pearl of great price' for me! Truly the Pearl found me, affirmed me, showing that He had never lost me. By His radical grace, I am gifted by the Holy Spirit to be an intercessor for His church and for His people. Time stood still at the conference those two days and the Holy Spirit broke loose in the hearts of all who would give Him entry."

As Lisa said, the Lord does not permit us to camp out on the mountaintop. After a few weeks when things returned to normal, the enemy of her soul started whispering, "See, nothing's changed, you still don't fit in." As the shadows began to fall over her joy, Lisa's rector came to her, saying that the Lord had impressed upon him to ask her to be the point person for intentional intercession in their church. God's timing was perfect.

Lisa concluded with a wonderful insight for all of us who pray and pray and can't seem to hear what God is saying:

"Stay on His bus; your ticket is punched. In due time your gift shall make room and you shall fit. And that's a promise!"

Heart to Heart

Hanging above my desk is a card that reads, "Faith is the confidence that God has your best interests in mind when He answers No to your prayers." Living into this understanding of faith has taken years, decades. Like my children who used to cry, "You don't love me!" when I denied their request for candy, it's so easy to believe that God is withholding His love when He withholds our requests. And yet, God knows us better than we know ourselves — often He denies us the candy because He knows He's about to serve us a hearty meal.

When we get to the deepest level of prayer, what we request becomes secondary — we are in the presence of God and that is enough. At that place, we are heart to heart with the Creator of the universe. Nothing else matters.

One day, we will be heart to heart with God forever, praising Him throughout eternity. In the meantime, however, we have all sorts of staggering as well as niggling things that snag and consume our attention away from prayer. And yet, Paul tells us in the Bible to pray without ceasing. So, how to reconcile prayer and plumbing problems?

Stream-of-consciousness prayer is one way. Carrying God with us in the car, at work, in the grocery store — bringing everything before Him as we push the cart through the vegetable section. It's part of our humanness to have a constant inner dialogue and we can bring up a chair for God as we make all our comments to ourselves about our daily lives.

I interviewed one woman, Lana, asking her if she had any stories about the ways God has worked in her life. She responded, "How many ways has He *not* worked in my life?" Clearly, this woman took God with her everywhere she went. She related a recent story as just one example. Lana is a computer guru, fixing problems from major shutdowns to minor glitches. She was working on a client's crashed computer and she had tried everything — to no avail. She started silently praying, and boom — she knew what to do.

Lana's trust in God through prayer extended to a lump she found recently in her breast. Through prayer and reflection, she felt so encompassed by God's love and was at peace that everything would work out as it should, even if the worst was diagnosed. "The hardest part of the ordeal for me was knowing that my family was so worried and upset."

Lana lives her prayer life, working not to become overly invested in the outcome but rather in the process. She concluded by saying, "All roads lead to prayer."

Often life has to take us to the very bottom of our own resources before we can turn to God in a heart-to-heart prayer. Nancy told this story about a disastrous turn of events in her life: Trapped in a vicious lawsuit over the rights to a summer camp she and her friends had built up over the course of many years, she came face-to-face with an unjust man who threatened to take away her campers, her reputation, her livelihood, her life's work, and her financial security. During an extended period of excruciating legal disputes, she found herself waking up at night, her heart pounding, terrified her whole life would fall apart in a heap of failure.

Nancy said, "I knew I was a child of God and that He was with me even in my panic attacks. I would sing 'Alleluia' until I fell back asleep." She paused. "Only later I found out that a group of nuns across the country knew about my situation and were praying around the clock for me." She was overwhelmed.

When Nancy started a new camp with a booming group of campers, she gave a talk on Sunday at the camp's chapel about giving thanks in all circumstances.

Lynn told a story of how God led her to the very bottom before healing her: "I had lost my job. My children were in the throes of teenage misery. I had a car wreck. Our house was falling apart. With each new disaster, I prayed. No answer. Then, I fell and broke my rib cage and was forced to sit in a chair by the window and just pray and read. All other activities hurt too much.

"That chair saved my life, my inner life. I thought of my broken rib cage as symbolic. The structure that had protected me and held me intact all my life had cracked and I needed God to provide me with a stronger structure. It was time to let Him be my life's structure in the deepest sense. So I sat still as He knit my rib cage and my life back together."

She concluded, "Now I'm back going a hundred miles an hour with two teenagers and a new job. I look back on those weeks of deep prayer as the most special thing that's ever happened to me. One day, as my children leave home and I retire, I hope I'll be able to spend more and more time in that chair by the window."

Teresa told the story of her mother's cancer and journey home. After being in pain for a year, her mother was finally diagnosed with cancer of the liver with a prognosis of six months to a year. Teresa said, "My foremost concern was facing life without her, a frightening prospect. After a distant and rocky past, we had come to a lovely place of being together, although we had an unspoken agreement not to discuss our religious differences. After hearing the news of her condition, my second and frightened reaction was for her salvation.

"My mother was raised Catholic. Like many in the Mexican and Mexican-American community, her fervency for tradition and ritual was handed down from my grandmother. When I was saved through means other than the

Roman tradition, she felt stung by betrayal and became unresponsive to my spiritual life."

Teresa continued, "The evening I heard the news about her cancer, I knew I had to speak to her about the unspeakable. I remember being in the shower crying before God and confessing that I had not been sensitive enough to her feelings on the subject and fearing that my own ego would lead her further away from accepting the saving act of Jesus' death and resurrection. I had painted myself in a corner unknowingly by my aggressive agenda of converting my mother on my new religious terms and had no idea how to get out. I cried before God, shameful and broken, with full recognition of my stupidity and arrogance. And then the Lord whispered in an inaudible voice that everything would be all right. 'Fear not' repeated itself over and over in my heart. I was washed with an indescribable peace that I will never forget. I promised the Lord that I wouldn't make another move until I knew without a doubt that I was being prompted by His Spirit."

Teresa's mother continued with medical procedures, one that gave her relief from pain for several months. Coming out of the hospital, she reported a dream she had about St. Peter. Teresa said, "I sensed a gate swinging open as if I were to walk through it. I told her that God shows His love for us through our circumstances. It was only a few sentences, then I felt the gate closing. I had to pull back and allow God to work.

"Her condition deteriorated. In one of her last moments of alertness, my brother sat with her and told her that Christ died so she might live. She was blind by then and unable to speak. He explained it was not by works that we enter heaven, but by God's grace. She responded with small nods. Her last nod was to accept Jesus as her Lord and Savior. She slipped into a coma and died less than twenty-four hours later."

In her heart-to-heart time with God in the shower, Teresa became a part of her mother's salvation, planting seeds that later carried her mother into the Kingdom of Heaven.

When All Else Fails Try Prayer and Endurance

St. Augustine was born in 354 in what is now part of Algeria. Though she was the wife of a pagan, his mother, Monica, signed him with a cross when he was born and made sure he had a Christian education. Monica prayed for both her husband and her son to become Christians.

Monica's husband was baptized before he died in 371. Augustine was fifteen or sixteen at the time, but his journey to faith took another seventeen years. At one point, Monica was so distressed at her son's lifestyle that she was tempted to refuse him at her table. However, she was talked into a patient and prayerful path by a wise bishop.

Shortly after his father's death, Augustine joined the Manicheans. Monica prayed. After a few years, Augustine left the Manicheans and toyed with other philosophies. Monica prayed. Augustine made an alliance with a woman who bore him an illegitimate son. Monica prayed. He moved to Rome. Monica followed him, praying.

Augustine inched toward seeing the light. He asked God to make him holy, but "not yet," because he didn't want to give up his mistress. Year in and year out for those seventeen years, his mother prayed for God to show His face to her son.

When Augustine finally converted to Christianity, he became Bishop of Hippo and one of the major patriarchs of the faith. His theology has impacted the church for sixteen hundred years; his spiritual autobiography, the *Confessions*, is a classic that still touches the lives of believers.

Monica also became a saint, an exemplar for her faithfulness in prayer.

Long-term prayer projects fall into different categories, not just wayward adult children but elderly parents whose bodies live on after their minds are gone, alcoholic spouses, friends who continue to reject the love of God. From the parents' point of view, the teenage years seem like an unending desert of prayer. Parents often see the wonderful things God has in store for their kids, but the teens aren't ready to accept His will yet. Pointing out God's love is received with eyeballs rolling back and "Yeah, yeah, yeah, we know, Mom." Dragging them to church leaves heel marks in the carpet. So the only thing left is prayer — and the realization that the Holy Spirit's timing is perfect, while ours is not.

At one time or another most of us have reached the point when well-meaning advice and friendly reminders (oh, all right, call it nagging) have produced a roadblock, or resentment, instead of the eureka moment we all hope for. Of course, praying is what we should be doing from the start, but most of us sometimes try to work out the situation on our own.

Beverly's mother had been diagnosed as a bi-polar alcoholic with borderline personality disorder. She said, "You can just imagine what growing up with her was like. When I was in my mid-thirties, my brother and I took our mom to a treatment center for her alcoholism. It was rugged. She resisted.

"After that, I realized that barring a serious miracle, her healing probably wasn't going to happen. I also realized that, although I needed to continue to pray for her, I needed to pray for my own healing because the wounds were deep and crippling. I had to stop blaming her. I had to stop trying to will myself to overcome these problems. Prayer was the most powerful tool to combat this deep-seated stuff. From treatment, I learned that if I didn't get healed myself, then I'd simply pass on the problems to the next generation."

Beverly continued, "For fifteen years I prayed to be released from the demons of fear, anxiety, anger, failure, and depression — the legacy of my mother. She has continued to spin like a whirling dervish, and contact with her still triggers all the negative horrors within my psyche. Yet God began a slow, slow process of healing. Gradually, year by year, I got better until finally, during one vacation with the family, I knew I was healed. My mom is still a problem to be around, but at least I can honor her and feel compassion for her.

"It may take another fifteen years, or my mom may die still caught up in all her diseases, but I know that God will heal her sooner or later, either on earth or in heaven. In the meantime, her healing is my constant prayer."

A grandmother tells the story of her daughter, Katherine, and her grandson, Jake. As Jake approached school age, he was having trouble learning to read, a problem that grew worse and worse. Years later, long after his classmates had progressed beyond him, he still could not read at all.

Books were very important in Katherine's family and she grew increasingly anxious over her son's inability to read. When the grandmother would compliment Jake with something special she had noticed about the child, Katherine would respond, "Yes, but he can't read."

"He's wise beyond his years," said Grandmother.

"But he can't read," said Katherine.

"He notices what people need and helps them," said Grandmother.

"But he can't read," said Katherine.

The grandmother began to see that Katherine's fixation on Jake's inability to read was undermining Katherine's own ability to see the gifted and precious boy that Jake was. The grandmother began to pray. For more than five years, she prayed daily that her daughter would learn to love Jake unconditionally.

Then, at a twelve step meeting Katherine met and was drawn to a woman named Susan who had a special intuitive gift. Katherine called her when she got home. Though the two women knew nothing about each other, Katherine asked Susan to tell her what she sensed about Jake, an eight-year-old boy in Katherine's life. That's all the information she revealed about him.

Without hesitation, Susan said, "Jake is a very wise little boy, wise beyond his age. He sees past the obvious. He will never be like others."

Katherine responded, "But he can't read."

Susan said, "He doesn't need to read. Reading is not as important as his other gifts. He will be able to read what he needs to in order to do what God calls him to do. Katherine, you are to love him like he is. Love him unconditionally."

Katherine finally heard from Susan what she had not been able to hear from her mother. Excited, she called her parents. God had lifted a great weight from her heart and she felt a hint of what God's unconditional love must feel like for Jake as he is.

One young woman, Brianna, felt called to take on her grandmother as a prayer project. Her grandmother had been active in church for most of her life, but when she was in her eighties, she lost a daughter to a drunk driver. Shortly after that, another daughter's husband, a minister, divorced her for a younger woman, leaving the daughter in dire straits. These two events wrecked the grandmother's faith in a loving God. She became an embittered old woman.

Brianna watched this happening and tried to talk with her grandmother on more than one occasion. Every time Brianna mentioned God, though, her grandmother turned into stone and changed the subject. Brianna stopped bringing up religion, for fear she would do more harm than good. Instead, she prayed for her grandmother.

Her grandmother lived for another thirteen years, un-budging in her bitterness toward God. At her funeral, the minister simply said, "She is in God's hands." Brianna said, "The minister is right. God knows how wounded and be-trayed she felt. Even Jesus on the cross felt betrayed by God, so I can only pray that God understands her hurt and forgives her for it." Brianna paused, then added, "Some-times, we don't get to see the results. We just have to have faith."

Angie told the story of her son, Kevin, who had scored in the top 99 percentile on the SAT and had been admitted to Cornell. He wanted to be a brain surgeon. Then one day he couldn't get out of bed. He'd missed a deadline for class and was confused about how quickly time had gone by. A conscientious, motivated young man, he was deeply troubled by his own behavior. He took two medical leaves from school, but eventually had to drop out from a nervous and mental breakdown.

Angie said, "Little did I realize that Kevin had inherited a mental illness from his father's side of the family. His father died when Kevin was younger, and I didn't know until now that two of his first cousins had committed suicide. A third relative had been troubled by this same mental affliction, but she had been sheltered at home and no one knew the extent of her illness because she had successfully raised two children and had three grandchildren."

Kevin is now in his late forties, still under care and medication and so far unable to live independently. Angie said, "I cannot abandon my son. I cannot put him away." In spite of her son's debilitating condition, Angie thanks God for him every day. She takes it one day at a time, keeping 1 Peter 5:10 in the forefront of her mind: "And the God of all grace, who called you to his eternal glory in Christ, after you have suffered a little while, will himself restore you and make you strong, firm and steadfast."

Strong, firm, and steadfast. Angie has accepted her son and her situation. Death would have provided a finality; instead, she is faced with a "living grief," in many ways a much more difficult trial than death. Yet she remains firm in her faith and knows that her prayers will see them both through.

Sometimes it's the long-term prayers that can discourage us — nothing seems to change. Yet even if the circumstances seem unaltered, we can rest knowing that we are growing, as slowly and imperceptibly as a blossom, into the love of God.

 # The Purpose of the Journey

In the final analysis, we will be called home and all mysteries will be revealed. In the meantime, often we ask what the point of the whole trip is. As women we spend our days making choices — what to do, who to be. We create and sustain relationships; we work through lists of things to do, taking deep breaths and relaxing when we can. Our lives take some pretty strange turns. And what, we continue to ask, is the purpose of the journey?

The story of a woman named Esme sums up a great deal. Esme worked on Capitol Hill in Washington when she met her husband, a seminarian. They married and she worked in public relations for a hospital and taught for fifteen years, creating her own evangelism curriculum called Equipping the Saints. She raised two beautiful and intelligent children, and when they entered high school, she ran two political campaigns. Now, after a balancing act for seventeen years, she has been called for full-time work at a national level for her church's denomination.

Esme provided several insights I'd like to conclude with. When she went back to work full-time, her college-age daughter watched her: "Mom, you're so different. I didn't realize who you really are." She saw her mother as strong, as an individual, not merely as an adjunct to her father. "I want to be like you," she told Esme.

Esme said, "I agonized over the decision to go back full time. But God has shown me that we can be faithful to more than one thing. This is different from embracing the 'Super Woman' model. If God asked me to quit tomorrow, I would."

The second insight Esme offered is based on something a man said to her after a class she taught at church. People often told her that she'd done a good job, but an older man came up to her and said, "After listening to your class, I have made a major life decision. God spoke to me through your class." Esme said, "I find it a constant miracle that God can use me — as me. That He prepared me through all my experiences for what He wanted me to do. With my difficult and painful family background, it's been hard to accept that He has a plan just for me."

She continued, "It's not about being comfortable, but about being faithful."

I have heard our life spans on earth described in a variety of metaphors: If life is a journey, then we travel over rough roads and smooth highways along with our fellow travelers. If life is a landscape, then we cover hills and valleys. If life is a pie, then we have some slices that are tasty and some that are rotten. If life is a plot of land, then we till and harvest and try to keep the garbage dump in a far corner.

Whatever metaphor we choose, life offers both suffering and joy. The purpose of our time here isn't about happiness or comfort. It's coincidentally about love, obedience, and helping others, but primarily it's about our relationship with God. Beginning now. Never ending.

Our life on earth is preparation for Heaven (a Kingdom we don't fully understand); lasting for eternity (a concept we can't conceive); serving a Lord (whose love is unfathomable). It's no wonder we so often feel that we stumble instead of glide through life. Yet everything that happens to us here contributes to our readiness for the Kingdom of Heaven. That is the purpose of our time on earth.

As women and co-creators of life, we are close to the heartbeat of existence. We know the painful cost of all life — from birthing children to burying them. As Mary bore the Son of God and returned to the tomb to anoint His body, so we bear Christ in each others' lives, sharing also in His resurrection.

Our church projects, our families, our friends, our circumstances, our joys, and our pain are all collected into the big basket we bring to Jesus' feet. Prayer is the answer to the question. We are put on the earth to be in relationship with God through Jesus Christ and the Holy Spirit. Short prayers, group prayers, spontaneous prayers, unlikely prayers, and long-term prayers — we offer the totality of our lives to Jesus.

It's the basking in His love, the asking for forgiveness, the begging for His presence in times of difficulty, the offering up of our family and friends in need — it's the conversation that will keep going when we leave the kingdom of earth and enter the Kingdom of Heaven.

What are we here for? We have the glorious opportunity to participate as God builds the Kingdom, through us and through our prayer — now and for eternity.

Acknowledgments

This book has revealed to me how rich I am in friends and family, and how blessed I am to share the Christian journey with so many gifted and wonderful Kingdom-builders. Thank you to the women who have made this project possible, whose stories fill these pages: Lakota Abbott, Judy Alban, Judith Allison, Moira Attwell, Judy Bauer, K. Leah Bellamy, Laurie Bourne, Bea Brock, Jane Brown, Cindy Brust, Kathy Bryson, Becky Casey, Sue Chambers, Kathryn Clark, Beverly Conine, Meredith Cooper, Jo Ann Dickinson, Mary-Keith Dickinson, Rita Nell Diffie, Cel Dryden, Joan Dunham, Jean Eastes, Gina Fugate, Betty Fuller, Betty Gaston, Jenness Gilles, Antoinette Hamilton, Patricia Herd, Laquita Hoover, Katherine Howe Frilot, Bonnie Hubbard, Kristin Huffman, Beth Johnson, Terry Jolliffe, Linda Kelly, Elizabeth Loggie, Jane McAbee, Elaine Magruder, Anne Nicholson, Nicia Oakes, Judy Parker, Amye Phillips, Karen Poidevan, Dee Popp, Alison Porter, Lorean Pulley, Darlynna Rush, Molly Sharpe, Catherine Schulte, Laura Scott, Vicky Shaw, Jane Swartz, Pat Templer, Pat Thames, Dana Turner, Melissa Wampler, Brandy Weatherford, Rebecca Williamson, Sue Wright, and those who wished to go unnamed. A special thank you goes to Rosemary Katsaras, one of God's most delightful children, who worked for many years building the Kingdom on earth, and who now (I'm quite sure) is regaling those in the Kingdom of Heaven with her stories and her love.

I'd like to thank my prayer group for their prayers, wisdom, strength, and humor — Bea Brock, Carole Hovde, Waynoka Lawrence, Anne Williamson, and Judy Parker from afar. The staff at the Crossroad Publishing Company has been great. I'd like to thank the SC for doing such a splendid job in tightening the prose and making sure that the sentences make sense. Most of all, I'd like to thank Roy M. Carlisle, Senior Editor, who has had a vision of this book for a long time and who guided me every step of the process. His editorial gifts are truly inspired, and he is a delight to work with.

Seeing a book from beginning to end is not always an easy — or even rational — process. My family, and especially my husband, deserves special thanks — for patience, for listening, for putting up with the highs and the lows of translating experience into words. My family has loved me through it all, and I am deeply grateful.

Finally, those of us involved in creating this book understand that we are not the ones building the Kingdom at all, but rather that it is God who builds the Kingdom through us. Since God is the main character here, all stories are told under different names. As an ancient poet said, we are holes in the flute through which Christ's breath moves, and my prayer is that the Holy Spirit will make music through these stories. Thanks be to God. Amen, Amen.

About the Author

Leslie Williams lives in Kerrville, Texas, where she teaches English through Midland College's statewide distance learning program. She is married to Stockton Williams, an Episcopal priest, and they have two teenage children, Jerre and Caroline. Leslie and Stockton have established a non-profit organization, Building the Kingdom Ministries, Inc., which runs a retreat center and restaurant called St. Martha's Hideaway. All proceeds from the book will go toward St. Martha's Hideaway.

A Word from the Editor

In 1996 I had the privilege of being part of a very creative leadership team of publishing folk, all women except for me. Out of that mix emerged a book that had its own day in the sun and became a small part of publishing history in the US. It sprang forth from the fertile mind of Julie Bennett, a marketing maven who had an uncanny ability to capture the feeling tone of other women, and it was written by two incredibly talented women, Tamara Traeder, a lawyer by training but a writer by temperament, and Carmen Renee Berry, noted therapist and already a bestselling author in her own right, and eventually *girlfriends* found its way onto the *New York Times* bestseller list and stayed there for 52 weeks.

At the heart of the book was the wisdom of dozens of women who had been interviewed about their relationships with other women. The beautiful packaging, the postmodern format (no chapters and short essays easily read in any order), and the way the interviews were used, were all distinct elements that led to more than 1.5 million copies of the book being sold. The media storm that occurred during the sales run of *girlfriends* provoked an idea in me which has taken nine years to bring to fruition. The wild success of that book made it very clear that women's relationships were incredibly important to women themselves but also to the culture as a whole.

I began to look for someone who had the time and ability to catch my vision for a book that would also capture that same dynamic among women of Christian faith. But with a twist. I wanted a book that portrayed the unique contribution that women of faith bring to the building of relationships (and thus the Kingdom of God) and to the enlargement of the ministry of the church universal. I talked to several writers who, for one reason or another, could not take on the task of producing the book that I wanted to publish. Then I met Leslie Williams.

I distinctly remember our first conversation while sitting in chairs in Paula D'Arcy's home in Kerrville, Texas. Leslie is an articulate woman of faith and erudition. She has a Ph.D. in literature and comes from a heralded family of writers. Many options were discussed that day. Not this specific project, but the groundwork was laid for something else to emerge out of our collaboration.

Some months later I began to revisit my desire to publish this book on women building the kingdom. Sitting in my little alcove of an office in my former home it occurred to me that Leslie had all the necessary talents to do a book like this. So I called to suggest this idea one more time to another woman writer. I was prepared to be turned down again since that had become the standard response. To my deep pleasure Leslie responded positively and we were on our way. Intuitively she understood what I wanted and it fit with her own perceptions of what might be viable as a book.

And what might be really helpful for encouraging women to take heart at the nature of their distinct ministries and to celebrate their amazing contributions to the Kingdom.

Allow me to be quite clear. This is Leslie's book. Having an *idea* for a book is one thing and I don't want to diminish that part of the process. But Leslie built this book from the ground up and she deserves full credit for its readability, its whimsy and humor, and its intelligence and sanity. I commend her as a woman who also actively involves herself in ministry and as a woman who brings her skill and wisdom to her writing. This is the book I wanted for nine years and I am proud to now see it in your hands. I salute all women who so sacrificially and lovingly build the Kingdom for all of our sakes.

Roy M. Carlisle
Senior Editor

Of Related Interest

Paula D'Arcy
WHEN PEOPLE GRIEVE
The Power of Love in the Midst of Pain

Since the publication of her first bestseller, *Song for Sarah*, Paula D'Arcy has become an internationally renowned expert in grief and bereavement issues. Now in a completely revised and updated version of an earlier book, Paula helps us understand how to cope with the process of grief and also how to reach out to others in the pain of grief. This classic manual is full of practical advice.

Paula D'Arcy, author of the bestsellers *Gift of the Red Bird* and *Sacred Threshold*, is a former psychotherapist and president of the Red Bird Foundation. She is a frequent speaker in Europe and the United States and lives in northern California.

crossroad